Hodder & Stoughton

A MEMBER OF THE HODDER HEADLINE GROUP

Orders: please contact Bookpoint Ltd, 78 Milton Park, Abingdon, Oxon OX14 4TD. Telephone: (44) 01235 400414, Fax: (44) 01235 400454. Lines are open from 9.00–6.00, Monday to Saturday, with a 24-hour message answering service. Email address: orders@bookpoint.co.uk

British Library Cataloguing in Publication Data
A catalogue record for this title is available from The British Library

ISBN 0 340 790 46 6

First published 2001
Impression number   10 9 8 7 6 5 4 3 2 1
Year   2005 2004 2003 2002 2001

Typeset by Transet Limited, Coventry, England.
Printed in Great Britain for Hodder & Stoughton Educational, a division of Hodder Headline Plc, 338 Euston Road, London NW1 3BH by Cox & Wyman, Reading, Berks

CONTENTS

CHAPTER 1: WHO WAS LEONARDO DA VINCI?   1
The 'Renaissance Man'   1
Famous biographers of Leonardo   3
Leonardo's early life and family   4
Summary   7

CHAPTER 2: THE RENAISSANCE   8
The 'rebirth'   8
History of the Renaissance   9
The Early Renaissance in Florence   12
The High Renaissance in Florence   15
The Late Renaissance   17
Summary   17

CHAPTER 3: LEONARDO IN FLORENCE 1469–81   18
Florence during the Renaissance   18
The Medici family   19
Leonardo's apprenticeship to Verrocchio   20
Working from nature   22
Some early works   24
The theme of Madonna and Child   26
Two unfinished pictures   27
Summary   28

CHAPTER 4: MILAN UNDER THE SFORZAS 1482–99   29
The Duchy of Milan   29
Leonardo's private life   31
Leonardo the engineer and architect   32
Leonardo the musician   34
Leonardo the painter   34
The Sforza monument   37
Summary   38

CHAPTER 5: TROUBLED TIMES 1500–7   39
Leonardo the traveller   39
Return to Florence   41
Travels with Cesare Borgia   44
Leonardo the cartographer   45
The Battle of Anghiari   46
Summary   48

CHAPTER 6: LEONARDO'S NOTEBOOKS I   49
The jottings of a genius   49
The organized cosmos   50
Amazing machines   53
Flight   55
Stories and reflections   56
Summary   60

CHAPTER 7: LEONARDO'S NOTEBOOKS II   61
The arts   61
Observing the natural world   63
Optics and perspective   66
Anatomy   68
Composition   70
Summary   71

CHAPTER 8: THE FINAL YEARS 1508–19   72
Back to Milan   72
Elaborate projects   73
Rome   74
Last works   76
At the French Court   77
Summary   78

Contents

TIMELINE 1452–1519	79
GLOSSARY	80
FURTHER READING	83
WHERE TO SEE LEONARDO'S WORK	84
INDEX	85

Who was Leonardo da Vinci?

Leonardo da Vinci was one of the most important figures of the **Renaissance**, and one of the
greatest geniuses that has ever lived. He was
born near Vinci, Italy, in 1452 and died in
France in 1519.

THE 'RENAISSANCE MAN'

Most people probably think of Leonardo first
and foremost as an artist and are familiar with
his most famous works such as the *Mona Lisa*.
His artistic achievements were outstanding,
not only in painting, but also in drawing and

KEYWORDS

Renaissance, a progressive
cultural period which
spanned the fourteenth to
sixteenth centuries. It was
characterized by a 're-birth'
of Classical thinking and a
huge growth of new ideas
in art, science, philosophy
and writing.

Esoteric, secret or mystical.

sculpture. But his interests extended far beyond the artistic field – he
was also an intellectual giant in the developing field of science and
much of his understanding was astonishingly ahead of his time. In fact
his interests were so diverse and advanced that he is often thought of
today as a kind of ideal image of 'Renaissance Man'. He explored
physics, mathematics, geometry, anatomy, mechanics, geology, botany
and geography. Amazingly he was also an accomplished musician,
architect and engineer.

Leonardo was an illegitimate child who was raised in a large and
wealthy extended family. As such his education was largely neglected
and his vast range of knowledge was mostly self-taught. Right up to the
end of his life he retained a lively and interested mind and was always
hatching new schemes and ideas. Leonardo was fascinated by the natural and **esoteric** worlds with their myriad forms and symbols. His
paintings reflect his meticulous observations in many ways – his
human figures seem almost to come alive and he introduced many new
techniques into the field of art. Even the backgrounds of his pictures
are full of tiny details and complex symbolism. He has also left us a lot
of writing, but it is chaotic – he intended to collect his ideas together

into a coherent whole, but he never actually got round to it. This seeming disorder underlines the fact that he was an intuitive thinker, always leaping ahead to be interested in the next idea. Order and sorting were not his strong points – indeed he never finished many of his larger projects. Much time was taken up in his work as a military engineer, architect and designer and organizer of pageants and state occasions. Few works of art remain that are entirely and reliably attributable to him, and yet his influence upon the art world has been immense and can be seen in the work of many subsequent artists.

Of his personal life we know little – he was a private person in many ways, concerned mainly with his own affairs and with the endless questions posed by his restless, probing mind. He travelled widely and changed his allegiances when it suited him. 'Alone you are all yourself, with a companion you are half yourself' he wrote in one of his notebooks. Indeed he is often reported as having been aloof, cold and rather odd. Nevertheless he always seemed to have a few devoted pupils and

Order and sorting were not his strong points.

companions around him, and he was well known for his charm and offbeat sense of humour.

Leonardo always had a tendency to record his thoughts and ideas on scraps of paper and from about the middle of his life onwards he kept a series of notebooks. When he died, all his writing, amounting to thousands of pages, was collected together by his friend, Francesco Melzi. Some of this material was in leather-bound notebooks and some in loose bundles tied with string and ribbon. It was gradually dispersed to public and private collections all over Europe, and today the whereabouts of about half of it is known. It is from these pages that we can glean a lot of knowledge about the man who wrote them. Nearly every page has many sketches and detailed diagrams interspersed with tiny hand-written text.

FAMOUS BIOGRAPHERS OF LEONARDO

Most of what we know about Leonardo's life story is brought to us by various early biographers, most notably Giorgio Vasari (1511–74). There are others worth looking at as well – in particular Paolo Giovio and Anonimo Gaddiano.

Paolo Giovio (1483–1552)

Giovio was one of Leonardo's earliest biographers and he wrote a short account in Latin in about 1527. Giovio was a physician, so he was chiefly interested in Leonardo's scientific achievements, especially in the field of **dissection**. Leonardo emphasized that artists should have proper training in science and **anatomy**, so that they would understand what they were looking at – the muscles, bones and joints of the body and the ways in which they moved. Another important field of study was **optics**, where the student needed to consider light and shade and the effects of **perspective**.

KEYWORDS

Dissection, cutting up dead plants or animals in order to investigate the structure and functions of their parts.

Anatomy, science investigating the structure of animals and plants.

Optics, science investigating the eye and vision.

Perspective, the art of drawing solid objects on a two-dimensional surface in such a way that they appear solid and real.

The Anonimo Gaddiano

Gaddiano wrote a short description of Leonardo in 1530, which was also only a few years after Leonardo's death. He commented that Leonardo was physically very beautiful and also talented in many ways, but that he did not paint many of his ideas because his spirit was never still and he could never be satisfied with the results. Leonardo apparently wore a pink, knee-length robe, which was unusual considering the current fashion was for long ones, and his hair was long, curly and well cared for. Talents that Gaddiano mentions are maths, perspective, eloquent speech, playing the lyre, and the engineering of waterworks and fountains.

Giorgio Vasari (1511–74)

Vasari was a painter, art historian and biographer, who wrote about Leonardo 30 years after his death, which means that some of the reporting is probably not accurate. Nevertheless it is from Vasari that we get a lot of the enduring anecdotes about Leonardo's life. Vasari tends to idealize Leonardo, embroidering the stories of his life and making him into a sort of miraculous sage. 'Occasionally,' he says, ' in a way that transcends nature, a single person is marvellously endowed by heaven with beauty, grace, and talent in such abundance that he leaves other men far behind, all his actions seem inspired, and indeed everything he does clearly comes from God rather than from human art.' (Vasari, *Lives of the Artists.*) Clearly, for Vasari, Leonardo was the greatest of them all.

LEONARDO'S EARLY LIFE AND FAMILY

Leonardo was born on Saturday 15 April 1452 near the town of Vinci, not far from Florence. He was the illegitimate son of Ser Piero da Vinci, who was a notary – a lawyer. The da Vinci family had been important and well respected in the town since the thirteenth century. Although Leonardo was illegitimate his father took him into his household, where he was raised by his grandparents and by his Uncle Francesco. His father married four times and Leonardo eventually acquired 13 younger half-brothers and sisters, but the first of these did not arrive until Leonardo was 25.

Leonardo's natural mother was called Caterina, but it is not known for certain who she was, except that she seems to have been part of Piero's household. Soon after Leonardo's birth, she married a friend of Ser Piero called Antonio da Vinci, who worked at a nearby pottery. She then had five more children but left Leonardo to be raised by his father. Ser Piero worked in Florence most of the time, so Leonardo seems to have seen little of either parent. In addition, his illegitimacy barred him from going to university or entering the legal or medical professions.

Vinci was an old rural town, with a medieval castle, a church dedicated to Santa Croce, a scattering of houses, an inn and a town hall. Piero da Vinci's house was in the middle of the town, just across from the town hall. The name 'Vinci' refers to the rushes that grew on the banks of a local stream called the Vincio. Local country people used to weave and braid them, and later in life Leonardo tended to draw elaborate knot-work patterns in his notebooks and worked them into his paintings as a symbol of his name.

The local countryside provided wine, olives and flour. Leonardo's grandfather owned and worked an area of land and his uncle owned a mill, so he grew up close to nature, understanding the importance of wind, weather, the seasons and water. These became themes that were woven into his later work – in particular he was fascinated by botany, storms, and the movement of water. He had a great love of nature and would buy caged birds in the local market in order to set them free. Later in life he became a vegetarian, which must have been quite unusual in those days. His love of animals is also shown in a great skill with handling horses. Throughout his life he would closely observe the natural world and he was a true experimental scientist in that he believed that the only path to true knowledge was by careful observation and experiment. For him art and science went hand in hand – he used drawing as a way of observing, understanding and recording the things he discovered in the world around him.

Leonardo's paternal grandmother came from a family of potters near Vinci, who produced **terracotta** sculptures and decorated and painted **ceramics** such as tiles. Leonardo doubtless visited the pottery as child and would have been influenced by the objects and ideas that he saw there. He would also have visited local churches, many of which had artistic religious scenes and figures made of brightly painted wood.

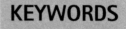

KEYWORDS

Terracotta, unglazed, brownish-red earthenware.

Ceramics, products made of clay and hardened by firing in a kiln.

One of the few tantalizing glimpses of childhood that we find in Leonardo's own notebooks is a recorded dream. In his dream, a kite (the bird of prey, not the child's toy) came down as he lay in his cradle and, opening his mouth with its tail, struck him many times between his lips (*Codex Atlanticus*). The famous psychoanalyst Sigmund Freud had a lot to say about this dream some 400 years later, maintaining that it held a clue to Leonardo's sexuality (more of which later).

From childhood, Leonardo seems to have been very volatile. He would begin projects only to get bored with them and quickly move on to something else. The boy grasped ideas astonishingly quickly – for example in arithmetic it took only a few months before he baffled his teacher with obscure questions. He learnt to play the lyre and accompanied his playing with improvised songs of his own. Meanwhile he showed an early talent for art and was always drawing, painting and modelling. Piero da Vinci was impressed by his son's efforts and eventually took some of his drawings to show to a friend of his, Andrea del Verrocchio, who was one of the foremost painters in Florence. Verrocchio was so struck by the boy's work that he suggested he joined his own workshop as an apprentice. The exact date Leonardo joined Verrocchio's workshop is obscure – usually young boys were apprenticed at age 12 or 13. Certainly he was living in Florence by 1469 and in 1472 he was inscribed on the roll of the Guild of St Luke as a painter.

We can divide Leonardo's life into three main phases:

* The first 30 years, spent in and around Florence.
* The next phase, 17 years in Milan.
* The last 19 years, where he had a restless, wandering existence in various parts of northern Italy and finally in France.

****SUMMARY****

* Leonardo da Vinci was one of the most important figures of the Renaissance.

* His genius was not only as an artist, but extended into science, engineering and music.

* He was born near Vinci in 1452 and grew up in a large family, living close to nature.

* We can learn about him through several early biographies and also through studying the numerous documents of his own that remain.

2 The Renaissance

THE 'REBIRTH'

The word 'Renaissance' comes from the French language and means 'rebirth'. It refers to the period of European history spanning the fourteenth to sixteenth centuries when many values and artistic styles from classical Greek and Roman times were revived. This revival gave rise to distinctive new styles in literature, music and the arts. The Renaissance was both a cultural and an intellectual movement and more recent scholars have tended to see it as heralding the birth of the modern age, bringing thinking out of the Middle Ages. Some of the characteristics of this new way of thinking were:

* Growth in scientific understanding as people began to develop the **empirical** method in order to observe and learn about the natural world.

* Increased geographical exploration and subsequent movements of population. The explorer Christopher Columbus was born a year before Leonardo.

* Emphasis on the importance of the individual – this emphasis gave rise to **humanism**. Humanist scholars studied Latin, Greek, grammar, **rhetoric**, poetry and history, as well as biblical and early Christian teaching.

* A shift in the focus of power away from religious authorities towards the **secular**.

* Art and literature began to be valued for their own aesthetic worth and as expressions of personal ideas. Before the Renaissance they had been used mainly as means to convey religious or moral messages.

HISTORY OF THE RENAISSANCE

The Renaissance began in northern Italy in the fourteenth century when lawyers and notaries began to study classical heritage. It gradually became the in thing to study Latin and classical ideas, especially law, architecture, art and history. Because most people were very poorly educated this learning helped some to gain promotion in high society careers in local government and in the Papal court at Rome. The rest of Europe lagged behind and things did not really get going until the fifteenth century when scholars from other countries such as France, Spain, England and Germany gradually came to Italy to study art, literature and the classics.

Italy had no central government as such at this time – the whole of northern Italy was divided into over a dozen competing and frequently despotic regional states, each with its own governing city. For example, Milan controlled Lombardy, Rome the Papal States, Florence and Sienna controlled Tuscany and Venice the Northeast. The men of power were

A great way of showing off how successful one was.

rich merchants who became great patrons of the arts, partly because it was a great way of showing off how successful one was.

For example they would commission vast and showy memorials, or give generous donations for art work in their local churches to show how pious they were. One of the most notable families was the Medici family, who held sway in Florence when Leonardo arrived there in 1469 (see Chapter 3).

There was a gradual expansion of intellectual thinking, encouraged by the ongoing more flexible, humanistic approach. People became interested in **philosophy**, medicine, physics and mathematics. The experimental approach to science began to evolve, particularly in fields such as anatomy, astronomy and **alchemy**. Special study was made of both ancient and more recent thinkers such as:

KEYWORDS

Philosophy, a system of learning that investigates the underlying nature and truth of knowledge and existence.

Alchemy, an esoteric practice combining aspects of mysticism, magic, science and religion.

Logic, the philosophy of reasoning.

Metaphysics, the philosophy of mind and thought.

Geometry, branch of maths that studies points, lines, surfaces and solid shapes.

Aristotle (384–322 BC)
A Greek philosopher and writer, who studied and taught **logic**, physics, **metaphysics** and biology.

Galen (c. AD 131–201)
A physician and writer, born in Asia Minor of Greek parents. He increased his knowledge, especially of the brain, nervous system and circulatory system, by experiments and dissections. He was the first to show that arteries carried blood, not air as had been previously thought.

Euclid (c. 300 BC)
A Greek mathematician who developed many ideas about **geometry**.

Plato (427–348 BC)
A Greek philosopher who wrote extensively about law, natural science and the relationship between man and the **cosmos**.

Petrarch (1304–74)
An Italian poet and humanist who wrote a lot in Latin. He was a pioneer in the rediscovery of classical texts. He lived for many years in Provence, France, and was eventually crowned Laureate for Latin poetry in Rome. He had a great influence on poetry, especially on love poetry and the **sonnet** and he revived many of the poetic styles of classical Roman times. Petrarch was popular with many figures in the nobility and his success spurred many others on to study the classics and so curry favour in high places.

Giovanni Boccaccio (1313–75)
Another Italian poet and storyteller, a scholar of Latin, Greek and mythology. His famous 'Decameron', a collection of witty and sexy stories, set against the contrasting background of the Black Death, is a classic of Renaissance romance. Boccaccio was a humanist.

Lorenzo Valla (1407–57)
A humanist writer who spoke out against traditional scholastic values and encouraged the revival of classical Latin.

The period of history covered by the Renaissance had its darker side. Warfare was common and bloody as competing powers jockeyed for position. People seeking power meddled in dubious practices such as **necromancy**. Worst of all, in the middle of the fourteenth century, about a third of the population of Europe was wiped out by the Black Death (bubonic and pneumonic plague). European economy became chaotic as labour became scarce, and recovery was slow. People understandably felt frightened and insecure and there were many who had apocalyptic visions and saw human nature and even creation itself as being horribly corrupt.

KEYWORDS

Cosmos, the universe.

Sonnet, poem with 14 lines and a formal rhyme scheme.

Necromancy, magic involving assistance from the spirits of the dead.

The Renaissance is traditionally divided into three approximate phases:

* Early – up until about 1495.

* High – about 1495–1520.

* Late – about 1520 onwards.

Florence became the most important centre of all for the development of Renaissance thinking. This was mainly for political reasons – by the beginning of the fifteenth century the Duke of Milan had become very powerful and was trying to get control of all northern and central Italy. Florence determinedly held firm as an obstacle to his progress, and hence became known as the 'new Athens', because Athens had been a similarly powerful city state and centre of culture in ancient Greece. The visual arts in particular were very important to people, because they symbolized the Florentine Spirit. This concept went right back to Plato, who believed that the artist could become possessed by a divine spirit that would then inspire his work.

THE EARLY RENAISSANCE IN FLORENCE

Giotto di Bondone (c. 1267–1337)

Giotto was a Florentine painter and architect who is considered to be one of the most important figures in the history of European art. He was one of the first to begin painting in a more natural, lifelike way. Medieval art had tended to portray people as looking wooden and two-dimensional, but Giotto began to paint people who were softer, more fluid and alive, with expressive faces.

KEYWORDS

Fresco, watercolour painting done on a wall or ceiling while the plaster is still wet.

Altarpiece, work of art set above or behind the altar in a church.

Where colours had tended to be very bright, in particular red, blue and gold, Giotto began to introduce more natural shades. The backgrounds of his pictures were also more realistic, and he was one of the first painters to begin using perspective effects, so that the landscape and figures in a painting really began to appear to exist on different levels. He worked on many **frescoes** and **altarpieces** in local churches in Florence and other places such as Naples and Rome. Some of his work, which would have influenced Leonardo, can still be seen in Florence today. He was nominated as the chief architect for the Cathedral in Florence and before he died in 1337 he began work on the beautiful bell tower which still bears his name.

Donatello (c. 1386–1466)

Donatello was one of the greatest Florentine sculptors. He was greatly influenced by classical art and humanist ideas. His most famous sculpture, a bronze statue of David (1444–46) was the first freestanding life-sized sculpture of the Christian era. Donatello's figures are alive, with very real, expressive faces. For the first time since classical times, Donatello brought sculpture to life and gave his people individual personalities. For example, his statue of Mary Magdalene has a tormented, anguished expression that is strikingly modern. She still stands in the Museum of the Opera del Duomo in Florence. Many of Donatello's sculptures still survive in Florence and would have been studied by Leonardo.

Filippo Brunelleschi (1377–1466)

Brunelleschi was another Florentine, an architect who contributed to many of the most famous buildings in Florence. It was Brunelleschi who developed the idea of linear perspective, which helps to give the illusion of

KEYWORD

Vanishing point, the point at which receding parallel lines, seen in perspective, appear to meet.

space projected onto a flat surface. The key feature is the idea of a **vanishing point**. Any set of parallel lines shown receding in a picture appears to converge at this point. If the lines are shown perpendicular to the picture plane, then the vanishing point is on the horizon, in a position corresponding to the eye of the observer. Leonardo later used this concept to portray perspective in his paintings.

Examples of Brunelleschi's architecture can still be seen in Florence, for example in the striking red octagonal ribbed dome of the cathedral and at the Church of San Lorenzo. He was also responsible for the design of the foundling hospital, an elegant building with a series of arches along the front supported by columns. At the head of each column is a glazed terracotta **tondo**, in blue and white, showing a baby in swaddling clothes. These

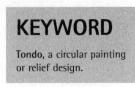

KEYWORD

Tondo, a circular painting or relief design.

are by another important artist, Andrea della Robbia. The orphanage was set up in 1419, at the expense of the Silk Worker's Guild. It is important not only as an example of the new style of civic architecture, but also because it reflects the growing humanistic concerns of the city.

Masaccio (1401–28)

Another artist who affected ways of looking at perspective was Masaccio. He was a painter and worked on the 'Trinity' fresco in Santa Maria Novella, Florence. He had a very good sense of proportion and the use of light and space to create a feeling of volume in a painting. People were beginning at this time to try to establish proper laws of proportion in architecture and in representing the human body. They had a tendency to over-do this, trying to work to a sort of ideal form, which actually tended to lead them away from observing nature. Leonardo was interested in these ideas, but he also valued painstaking observation of the natural world and the way people and things really looked. He delighted in creating grotesque caricatures, poking fun at

Leonardo loved to poke fun at people.

people in a satirical way that was not usually seen until later on in the history of art. 'The signs of the face,' he remarked, ' partly show the nature of men, their vices and their constitutions.' (*Codex Urbinas.*)

Antonio Pollaiuolo

The Pollaiuolos were a family of Florentine goldsmiths, painters, engravers and sculptors. Antonio Pollaiuolo ran one of the main Florentine workshops and was supposed to have been the first artist to study anatomy by means of dissection, a method much used later on by Leonardo.

Sandro Botticelli (c. 1444-1510)

Botticelli was another important Florentine Renaissance painter and a great favourite of the Medici family. Like his contemporaries he worked on religious and mythological scenes, such as the famous 'Birth of Venus' (1485–90), and 'Primavera' (1477–78), both of which are still in Florence, in the Uffizi gallery. He was a student of Fra Filippo Lippi, (c. 1406–69), who was also a very influential painter with a graceful and delicate style. Botticelli became a colleague and friend of Leonardo.

THE HIGH RENAISSANCE IN FLORENCE

From the mid- to the late fifteenth century there was an especially great revival and flowering of the arts in Italy, and Leonardo was born at just the right time and place to benefit from this and become part of it. As well as Latin, classical styles of sculpture, architecture, painting and modelling were all revived. By now the ideas of proportion and linear perspective were well established. The true style of the High Renaissance lasted for a brief period only (about 1495–1520) and was created by relatively few artists of great genius.

In many ways Leonardo was actually a man of his times and his thinking was typical of the era. For example, Renaissance thinking delighted in the use of **allegory**, subtle allusion, puns, jokes and secret symbols, all of which abound in Leonardo's work. Like Leonardo, many

KEYWORD

Allegory, story, poem, painting, etc., in which the meaning is represented symbolically.

Renaissance scholars saw both art and science as being important elements for the acquisition of knowledge. Leonardo actually regarded art as a science – the greatest of them all in fact. For him the painter was the lord of all thinkers, because whatever exists in the universe a painter can first visualize and then capture on paper.

Michelangelo Buonarotti (1475–1564)

Michelangelo was a Florentine sculptor, painter, architect and poet, whose influence was enormous. His character, like his sculptures, was colossal and dramatic and he was a great rival of Leonardo. He was a perfectionist and for him beauty was an expression of the divine. Many of his impressive sculptures, such as the powerful statue of David (1501–4) in the Galleria dell'Accademia in Florence, still survive. Like most artists of his day he worked on classical and religious themes. He impressed the Pope so much that he was commissioned to paint the ceiling of the Sistine Chapel in Rome, which is still considered to be the finest fresco in the world. Unlike Leonardo however, Michelangelo was not so interested in the natural, scientific world.

Raphael Santi (1483–1520)

Raphael was a painter who spent some of his time working in Florence. His work shows clear examples of the striving towards perfect harmony and balanced composition that so many Renaissance artists tried to achieve. This manifests in the way graceful human figures are arranged in the picture and also in carefully contrived perspective effects, with elaborate architectural details shown in the background. Raphael was influenced by Leonardo, and learned a lot from him about portraying emotion, using facial expression, movement and body language. He painted a whole series of Madonnas with sweet expressions, as well as many portraits. He also worked in Rome, where he was influenced by Michelangelo.

Niccolo Machiavelli (1469–1527)

Machiavelli – philosopher, politician, writer and poet – was one of the great thinkers of the Renaissance and a friend of Leonardo. He was a very influential diplomat and acted as defence secretary for the Florentine Republic.

THE LATE RENAISSANCE

In 1527 Rome was sacked, leaving many artists without patrons, so that they had to move away to France, Spain, or other parts of Italy. New anticlassical trends gradually began in art and **mannerism** developed. Vasari, Leonardo's early biographer, was an artist of this school. The mannerists greatly valued elegance, style and grace, to such an extent that the people in their pictures were often elongated and their bodies shown in unnatural postures. Individual talent became increasingly important, as artists vied for position, all trying to win favour from influential patrons. The original spark of true genius characteristic of the High Renaissance was beginning to wear thin.

KEYWORD

Mannerism, style of Italian art characterized by elongated figures and twisted poses.

✳ ✳ ✳ ✳ *SUMMARY* ✳ ✳ ✳ ✳

● The word 'Renaissance' means 'new birth'. Renaissance thinking gave rise to major advances in science and new styles in art, literature and music.

● The Renaissance began in Italy and gradually spread to other parts of Europe.

● Florence was the main focus of Renaissance thinking in Italy.

● Many of the scholars and artists who lived in Florence influenced Leonardo's work.

3 Leonardo in Florence 1469–81

FLORENCE DURING THE RENAISSANCE

The economy of Renaissance Florence depended on rich merchant families who traded internationally, particularly in wool. There were also many skilful bankers. These powerful men gave generously of their resources to finance study and the arts, turning Florence into a beautiful and very prosperous city. There were 21 influential trade guilds, seven major ones and 14 minor, which offered the chance for their members to enter government office. The top guildsmen came mainly from noble families, who were the ones most able to sway opinion. When a young man like Leonardo entered a guild as an apprentice the length of his training would depend on individual needs and the master's own views. Each guild had different specifications about how long training should take.

The guilds represented a wide range of crafts-men such as painters, embroiderers, sculptors, goldsmiths, architects, astrologers, carvers and clockmakers. When Leonardo arrived in Florence it was a bustling hive of activity, exporting painting, **marquetry**, furniture, stained glass, wool, silk, leather, ceramics, carving and sculpture. Incredibly there were 40 workshops devoted to painting, 50 for engraving, 80 for inlaid and carved woodwork and 44 goldsmiths. All these workshops were busy producing everyday objects for ordinary people, as well as carrying out expensive commissions for the well-to-do both locally and abroad. Much of the decorative work involved religious themes and scenes from classical mythology.

> ## KEYWORDS
>
> **Marquetry,** decorative inlaid work using wood, ivory, etc.
>
> **Apothecary,** chemist who dispenses medicine and drugs.
>
> **Pigment,** colouring used as paint or dye.

Painters were associated closely with **apothecaries**, mainly because **pigments** were used by both. The 'confraternity', or guild of painters, had St Luke as its patron. Ancient tradition had it that Luke was a physician, and had also painted a portrait of the Virgin Mary. After becoming a guild member a young painter would often remain with his master, because it would be expensive to set up his own workshop. Leonardo remained with his master Verrocchio for many years and was hired to do various assignments.

THE MEDICI FAMILY

The Medicis were traditionally interested in artistic and spiritual ventures. In 1436 they had founded a community for meditation in a reconstructed Dominican Friary. Cosimo de Medici, then head of the family, had two cells reserved for his own private use and had frescoes painted on the walls to aid meditation. One of these, depicting the Adoration of the Magi, was painted by an assistant of Fra Angelico (c. 1400–50). Fra Angelico was a Florentine monk and painter who created peaceful religious scenes, intended as aids to religious meditation.

The most powerful individual in Florence when Leonardo arrived was Lorenzo de Medici, often called 'The Magnificent', who was by now head of the Medici family. He was a great statesman, writer and patron of the arts, and was lord of Florence from 1469–92. Lorenzo was an ambitious man, both for himself and for Florence. Two big religious festivals occurred every year and were important for cementing good relationships between state and Church. The first of these was the feast of St John the Baptist, who was the patron saint of the city. His feast was celebrated at midsummer, 21–24 June. The other was that of the Epiphany (6 January), which is by tradition the day on which the Magi, or wise men, arrived to worship the baby Jesus. There was a confraternity of the Magi in Florence and members organized an annual re-enactment of the story. This was also a favourite theme for paintings.

Lorenzo undoubtedly used events such as these and commissioned expensive works of art in order to express his own power. But he had also developed a genuine interest in art, literature and philosophy. Florence was not only a great centre for artistic talent – it was also the most literate city in Europe at this time. At the same time there was also a great revival of interest in classical architecture and many contemporary buildings show characteristic designs of inlaid marble. Lorenzo was a generous patron and a loyal friend of various talented artists and architects such as Verrocchio, who would work on projects for public and Church purposes as well as for private use.

LEONARDO'S APPRENTICESHIP TO VERROCCHIO

Andrea del Verrocchio (c. 1435–88), was a leading figure in Florence in the 1470s and ran one of the most influential workshops in the city. He was a versatile artist, working in silver, gold, bronze, copper, marble, terracotta, **stucco**, wood, **tempera**, oil and other media. Above all, Verrocchio excelled at sculpture and metalwork. He made the huge ball of guilded copper that still sits on top of the Duomo in Florence. He was a well-educated man, having studied science, architecture, geometry and music and so he was able to give his pupils a broad education.

Verrocchio made use of **chiaroscuro** (from Italian, meaning 'light/dark') in order to make his painting come alive. He was very interested

KEYWORDS

Stucco, type of plaster used for moulding and for coating surfaces.

Tempera, painting using a mixture of pigment and other substances.

Chiaroscuro, making a sense of 3D in painting by using light and shade.

Putti (singular putto), a naked child, especially a cherub or cupid.

Contrapposto, twisted pose.

in facial expression and painted and sculpted many young men with the type of enigmatic smile that was later to become a characteristic of Leonardo's style. Early in his training Leonardo worked on terracotta heads of women with dreamy, thoughtful expressions, and **putti**, which were in popular demand. Another terracotta head, of the young Christ, survives from this period, but it is not known whether it was by Leonardo or Verrocchio.

Verrocchio was fond of intricate interlacing patterns and these too are a common theme in Leonardo's work, appearing as flowing hair, complex knotwork and swirling whirlpools. Verrocchio also made great use of **contrapposto**, or 'twisted pose' (from Italian 'placed opposite'). This was a style originally developed in ancient Greece, where people were shown moving in spiralling, graceful poses, often balanced on one leg.

When he became apprenticed to Verrocchio, Leonardo was plunged into an intellectual climate full of great thinkers and influential artists. Workshops like Verrocchio's were places where such people would meet to exchange ideas. Leonardo would have met and been influenced by many people, such as:

Paolo Toscanelli
A great mathematician and geographer, whose ideas inspired Columbus. He was also an astronomer and astrologer: as yet the two fields of study were not separated. He worked as a court astrologer, advising about auspicious times for political decisions and warfare. Leonardo was later very critical of astrology.

Sandro Botticelli
(See Chapter 2.) Botticelli was a little older than Leonardo and worked for a while as an assistant in Verrocchio's workshop.

Antonio Pollaiuolo
(See Chapter 2.) Pollaiuolo did nude figures and pictures full of action. He was interested in anatomy and dissection, which were becoming an accepted part of an artist's training.

Pierro Perugino 1450–1523
An artist famous for his altarpieces. He probably trained with Verrocchio and was the teacher of Raphael.

Leone Alberti 1404–72
An architect, musician, historian, engineer and painter who was another example of a 'Renaissance man' because his interests were so widespread. He wrote a treatise on painting, emphasizing the technological and scientific aspects.

During his early training a painter's apprentice was a general dogsbody. For example he would be expected to perform tasks like sweeping the floor, mixing up pigments, preparing panels for painting and making

gesso. Meanwhile he would be trained in 'disegno' (design), a topic which covered both design and drawing and was considered to be an intellectual activity. Paper was becoming more readily available at this time and quite a lot of Leonardo's drawings have survived.

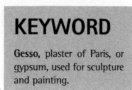

KEYWORD

Gesso, plaster of Paris, or gypsum, used for sculpture and painting.

Drawing was very important, not only for artistic training, but also as study and preparation for painting, and as a means of record keeping.

WORKING FROM NATURE

Today young painters often get little credit for being skilled draughtsmen and painters. If they produce a piece of work that has some resemblance to what has already been done, it is frequently scorned as being 'derivative'. In Leonardo's day things were very different for the young apprentice, who had to work devotedly for many years, carefully copying exactly what his master had done before him. In fact, when a master painter executed a commission, he worked only on the tricky and interesting bits. The apprentices did all the routine boring bits in exactly the master's style and nobody noticed the difference. This makes it difficult to decide which bits of a painting are attributable to which artist.

Leonardo, however, happened to be a person who was passionately interested in the world around him. The shapes of rocks and shadows, the action of rivers on the landscape, what ivy did to trees, how muscles moved the bones beneath the skin, the arrangement and shapes of leaves, the effects of gravity and air pressure – his sources of study were endless. This made his paintings more interesting and true to life because he knew more than most people did about what he was looking at. Leonardo emphasized that good master painters were hard to find and that it was probably best to go straight to nature for inspiration. Interestingly he remarked that an earlier painter, Giotto, had also not been satisfied with imitating the work of his master.

Verrocchio's pictures were not as realistic as Leonardo's. He was less imaginative and his colours were less subtle. From an early stage

Leonardo's work showed a characteristic use of muted colours – olive green, ochre and grey. The hands and faces of his people were delicate, almost dreamlike in quality, where Verrocchio's tended to be bold and firm, more earthly.

Leonardo's first known dated landscape drawing was produced in 1473 and is highly original. It shows the landscape of Santa Maria delle Neve and it is one of the earliest examples of landscape drawing in Western art. It is

KEYWORD

Sfumato, subtle model-ling of forms in painting, using gradual transitions of light and shade.

obvious that he must have done many other earlier drawings based on observation of the natural world because this is not the work of a beginner. The picture is full of detail and movement – tiny trees and bushes, foliage swaying in the breeze, water eddying and rushing and distant shapes of a castle and other buildings. This painstaking obser-vation was to become characteristic of his drawing and is found throughout his work. Before Leonardo, artists had tended to portray landscapes in a flat, dull, unrealistic and lifeless way, rather as if they were relating a story rather than looking at the living world. Leonardo introduced a whole new way of looking at things, using subtleties of light and shade portrayed by tiny strokes of brush and pen. He was largely responsible for the development of **sfumato** (Italian 'misty, softened'), a new technique made possible as oil paints were introduced. This involved subtle shading from dark to light, so elimi-nating sharp contours.

Leonardo's lively mind also took him frequently into worlds beyond our normal vision. There is a wonderful tale related by Vasari of the young Leonardo designing a terrifying monster, which he painted onto a figwood buckler belonging to a friend of his father (a buckler is a small round shield). In order to create the design, he carried into a private room 'a number of green and other kinds of lizards, crickets, serpents, butterflies, locusts, bats…to create a fearsome and horrible monster which emitted a poisonous breath and turned the air to fire'. (Vasari, *Lives of the artists.*) Right from the start Leonardo was clearly interested in the mysterious and magical – it is a pity that his fearsome beast has been lost.

A fearsome and horrible monster.

SOME EARLY WORKS

The Baptism of Christ (c. 1470–72, Uffizi Gallery, Florence)

This painting shows Christ being baptized by John the Baptist and it was commissioned by the Church of San Salvi in Florence. Verrocchio worked on it, assisted by Leonardo and possibly other pupils. The background may be Leonardo's – certainly it has a brooding, mysterious air to it, unlike the usual soft, rounded hills and dotted cypress trees that were in fashion, and it is painted with muted colours. On the left of the picture are two angels, one of which is attributed to Leonardo. Vasari says that when Verrocchio saw the quality of his apprentice's work he vowed that he himself would never touch paints again. The angel shows beautiful details in the drapery of his robes and in the cascade of his curly hair. The expression on his face is soft and dreamy, unlike the other angel, who looks rather fed up. Leonardo was especially fascinated by drapery and the effects of light and shadow in its folds. He would make clay figures and dress them in rags dipped in plaster. Then as they dried he would begin to draw the draped effects in black and white, using a brush on fine cloth or tinted paper.

The Annunciation (1470–75, Uffizi Gallery, Florence)

This picture depicts another popular biblical scene – the angel Gabriel is bringing the unexpected news of pregnancy to Mary. The background with detailed trees in silhouette against a grey-blue sky and a tiny harbour scene are again typical Leonardo. Although there are some mistakes in the perspective, showing that it was the work of a young artist, one can already see new ideas about depth effects being put to use. Things further away are shown as being smaller and mistier and there is a sense of a vanishing point somewhere on the horizon. In the foreground the artist has painted many flowers which seem to twist and grow from the page, unlike the usual regularly spaced artificial ones often seen in medieval art. Mary's face and body language are interesting too – Leonardo has managed to capture a moment in time and has shown her looking as if she is really paying attention to the angel's surprising announcement.

Soon after Leonardo became a master of the Painters' Guild of St Luke, which meant that theoretically he could set up as an independent painter. However, he stayed on at Verrocchio's studio until the late 1470s.

Ginevra de Benci (c. 1474, National Gallery of Art, Washington)

This was painted on the occasion of the subject's marriage and is one of Leonardo's first known portraits. Although it is not as natural as some of his later portraits, it certainly gives the impression that one is looking at a real person. The face is quite determined looking, possibly a little bored and condescending – the tight line of the mouth suggests someone rather unhappy. Much of the background is filled with the dark spiky leaves of a juniper bush, which represents a pun on the lady's name, 'ginepro' in Italian. This plant reappears on the back of the painting, in a garland with laurel and palm, accompanied by a little scroll that says 'beauty adorns virtue'. Leonardo's touch is also shown in the ringlets of her hair, the muted colours of her pale face and the grey and blue of the background.

THE THEME OF MADONNA AND CHILD

The theme of Madonna and Child was a very popular one and there are many variations, showing different aspects of the story. For example, some paintings show the young mother suckling the baby, another shows the child playing with a goldfinch, whose red face and habit of dwelling in thorny plants symbolizes the blood and agony of Christ's passion. Many drawings and sketches and several paintings of Leonardo's on this theme have survived.

Madonna with the Carnation (c. 1473–76, Alte Pinakothek, Munich)

This may be one of Leonardo's first independent works, but it is not certain whether he painted all of it – Verrocchio or another pupil may have contributed. Again there is symbolic use of natural imagery. Mary holds a red carnation, whose red, cruciform petals are symbolic of Christ's coming passion. The baby reaches for the flower with a strange expression, his eyes seeming to look up to heaven, rather than directly at the flower.

Benois Madonna (c. 1478–80, State Hermitage Museum, St Petersburg)

This is a delightful study, much more alive and human, which captures a moment of playful intimacy between mother and child. Leonardo captures the emotions of the young mother as she gazes intently at her child, who is reaching for a tiny sprig of white flowers, again with petals in the form of a cross. There are several sketches, which are probably studies for this painting, showing children playing with cats. These are clearly studies done from life and show how Leonardo used lightning-quick observation to get ideas down on paper as the subjects moved into different poses.

TWO UNFINISHED PICTURES

Saint Jerome Penitent (c. 1480, Vatican Library, Rome)

It is not known who commissioned this picture, or why. Like so many of Leonardo's projects, it remained unfinished. It is still in the stage of underpainting and so the colours are dark, mainly brown and golden yellows. The brighter colours would have been applied later on. St Jerome was an early figure of the Christian Church, about AD 370, who lived in the desert. He is shown beating his breast with a rock, his thin tormented face and knotted muscles giving an impression of tortured emotions and showing that Leonardo was becoming interested in anatomy. In front of Jerome is shown the lion who was his companion, and in the background is a distant building with sketchy architectural detail.

The Adoration of the Magi (commissioned in 1481, Uffizi Gallery, Florence)

Again, this is an unfinished underpainting and it shows a scene of extraordinary complexity. It is an outdoor scene with the Virgin and Child centre stage, surrounded by a bewildering mass of different figures in weird contorted poses. Some of them are wise men, paying homage with various gifts, but there are others, too – shepherds, perhaps, or angels. Some are reaching up to heaven, apparently completely awe-struck and amazed. Symbolism abounds in this picture, possibly more than in any other of Leonardo's surviving works. For example, one of the figures points heavenwards, in a gesture that became almost a trademark of Leonardo. On the right is an enigmatic young man who is turning his face away. People have suggested this may be a portrait of the poet Dante, or a self-portrait of the artist.

The background is even more bizarre, almost dreamlike or deranged. There is a huge ruinous building, with pillars and a staircase, round which is raging some sort of ferocious battle on horseback. Again several sketches exist which must have been studies for the picture, showing horses with shadowy riders, staircases and even a camel. The picture was commissioned as an altarpiece in 1481 by the Augustinian Convent of San Donato, but again it was never finished. This lends it an air of mystery, making it all the more fascinating, and also enables us to look at the way Leonardo built up a picture as he worked.

As well as working on various paintings, Leonardo was also showing wide and varied interest in other things. There are still huge collections of his drawings, the earliest of which date to about 1475 and show that he was taking an interest in engineering by this time. Again, he was a man of his time in that there were other engineers working in the region during this period, basing many of their ideas on classical and medieval sources. In 1478 Leonardo took on his first independent public commission, which was for an altarpiece in the chapel of San Bernardo in the town hall of Florence. He left Verrocchio's studio at about this time and set up on his own. Leonardo never finished this commission, and it was eventually completed by other artists. During this same year he probably also met Ludovico Sforza, Regent and later Duke of Milan, who was soon to become his patron and in 1481 Leonardo left Florence for Milan.

* * * *SUMMARY* * * *

- Florence was a busy and thriving cultural and commercial centre during the Renaissance.

- The Medicis, in particular Lorenzo the Magnificent, were very important patrons of the arts.

- Leonardo was apprenticed to Verrocchio, one of the leading Florentine artists, and remained in his workshop for many years.

- Leonardo gradually developed an individual style of his own, involving meticulous observation of nature and a love of mystery and symbolism.

Milan Under the Sforzas 1482–99

It is not clear exactly why Leonardo left Florence for Milan, but most likely he saw opportunities there that would be to his advantage. Lorenzo de Medici had always shown a rather lukewarm attitude to Leonardo's talents. At the Sforza court in Milan there were many doctors, engineers and scientists, all exchanging ideas, and Leonardo may have decided to change tack in order to get the recognition he needed. He composed a letter of application to Ludovico Sforza, extolling his virtues as a military engineer and architect. Almost as an afterthought he mentioned his talents as painter and sculptor, and offered to build a bronze equestrian monument to the head of the House of Sforza.

It is uncertain whether Leonardo ever actually sent this letter. Vasari says that Ludovico actually invited Leonardo to Milan in order to hear him play the lyre. He adds intriguingly that 'Leonardo took with him a lyre that he had made himself, mostly of silver, in the shape of a horse's head (a very strange and novel design) so that the sound should be more sonorous and resonant'. (Vasari, *Lives of the artists.*) With this cunning device and with his sparkling conversation he captured Ludovico's attention.

THE DUCHY OF MILAN

Ludovico Sforza, known as Il Moro ('The Moor' – on account of his dark complexion), ruled Milan between 1480 and 1499. He had a reputation for being vain, boastful and a despotic ruler, but he was a clever politician and managed to achieve a political balance between Milan, Florence and Rome. A lot of Milanese capital was invested into projects to do with land reclamation and canal building. Leonardo had always been fascinated by water and this early interest may have been aroused by the periodic flooding of the river Arno in and around Florence. Great artistic and cultural advances were also going on in

Milan and it was an important economic centre, exporting flax, textiles, glass, mulberries and rice. The mulberry was a traditional symbol of wisdom and prudence and it was adopted as an emblem by Ludovico's government. Clever symbols, mottoes, riddles and allegories were very popular. This fashion was encouraged by new advances in printing that meant that ideas achieved a greater circulation.

Ludovico emulated Lorenzo the Magnificent and tried to organize his court along classical lines. He was hugely ambitious, determined to make Milan as influential as Florence and establish the power of the Sforza line. The current power of Milan was based mainly on military strength. Skill in warfare was vitally

KEYWORDS

Pageant, an elaborate staged spectacle or parade.

Masque, dramatic and musical entertainment.

important and this meant that an engineer and inventor with such talents as Leonardo was offering could potentially be a great asset to Ludovico. But in fact Sforza did not employ court artists so Leonardo was not offered the salaried position at court that he coveted – he had to rely instead upon sporadic commissions. These included a lot of work connected with **pageants** and court entertainment, plus various artistic enterprises.

Leonardo was employed as a stage designer and musician at court for events such as wedding feasts and **masques**. In 1490 he organized the 'Festa del Paradiso', a grand pageant to celebrate the wedding of Isabella of Aragon and Gian Galeazzo Sforza, who was Ludovico's nephew. This took place at the ducal palace in Milan and included all kinds of marvels such as special sound and light effects, music and songs and mechanically animated heavenly bodies. This sort of thing was popular during the Renaissance – it was all part of the general flaunting of power and showing off.

Leonardo's notes from this period are an amazing hotchpotch of ideas – scientific diagrams are mixed in with sketches for war machines, costumes, heraldic emblems, jokes, riddles, puzzles, puns, mottoes, and odd snatches of music. All this makes it clear why he so seldom finished any commissioned paintings – his mind was constantly occupied with other distractions.

LEONARDO'S PRIVATE LIFE

Leonardo gradually became a successful and well-recognized painter during his time in Milan. In fact his two decades there saw the most successful part of his career. He founded a workshop, which produced sought after works of art, and began to gather admirers and students around him. He was proud of the fact that he was a self-made man, largely self-educated and he scorned many academics as prejudiced fools. Authority figures annoyed him as well, and when he did eventually accept commissions from Ludovico Sforza he showed a characteristic reluctance to be rushed or bossed about when he was creating works of art.

One pupil was to become very important in Leonardo's life. This was Giacomo Salai, a very good looking youth with abundant fair, curly hair. He first came to live with Leonardo in 1490 when he was only ten years old. Leonardo had two shirts made for him, a pair of hose and a jerkin. Salai was a bundle of mischief, telling outrageous lies and stealing money from Leonardo's purse – in fact he even stole the money that had been put aside for his own set of clothes. When Leonardo took him to dinner with a friend, Salai put away enormous quantities of food, broke three cruets and managed to spill the wine. Nevertheless he was definitely Leonardo's pet, and Leonardo never totally abandoned him, for he mentioned Salai in his will.

It is probable that Leonardo's relationship with Salai was a homosexual one. Homosexuality was common between master and pupil and Verrocchio was said to have been a practising homosexual, so Leonardo may well have been introduced to the idea from an early age. Back in Florence in 1476 Leonardo had been anonymously accused of homosexual acts, along with three other youths. The trial was dismissed for lack of evidence, but the experience would have had a lasting effect

Salai was a bundle of mischief.

upon the young Leonardo and would in part account for his rather secretive nature. Homosexuality was certainly common, but it was not well tolerated – in fact if you were tried and found guilty of it you could be burned at the stake. It seems likely that Leonardo was indeed homosexual – snippets in his notebooks suggest that he found the sexual act between man and woman rather repugnant. He had a lot of close relationships with handsome young men and he never married or was reported to have a female lover.

LEONARDO THE ENGINEER AND ARCHITECT

There are many plans in Leonardo's notebooks during this period for elaborate and terrifying war machines. This may seem rather strange when one thinks of him as a nature-loving vegetarian. In fact he detested warfare and referred to it as 'bestial folly'. But the times he lived in were harsh and people tended to take it for granted that life was short. Military power was where the money lay and Leonardo was certainly well aware of this and saw his inventions as a way to impress Ludovico.

In the summer of 1484, Milan was hit by an outbreak of plague. Leonardo lived through this, as he had an earlier outbreak in Florence, but it is likely that he would have lost some close friends, for upwards of 10,000 citizens died. Leonardo seems to have been aware that plague was spread because of cramped and insanitary living conditions. He gave much thought to planning an idyllic new city, with a proper sewage system, waterworks, roads and

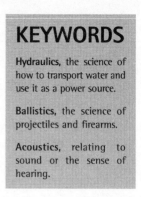

KEYWORDS

Hydraulics, the science of how to transport water and use it as a power source.

Ballistics, the science of projectiles and firearms.

Acoustics, relating to sound or the sense of hearing.

even machines for washing the streets. He developed a particular interest in **hydraulics** and devised all kinds of devices for pumping and transporting water. He became involved in many schemes, not only for sewage and city water supplies, but also in the countryside around Milan for irrigation, land drainage, locks and canals.

His notebooks show that Leonardo gave much thought to engineering related topics such as **ballistics,** optics and **acoustics.** He considered the ways in which forces acted upon physical bodies and how to devise systems for using them more efficiently. He invented machines such as looms, clocks, rolling mills and grinding machines, making meticulous notes and drawings (more about these in Chapter 6). With such wide-ranging genius he gradually became a respected problem solver to whom clients would come for advice. With other engineers he worked on a design for a dome for Milan cathedral from 1487–88, but like so many other projects this one was abandoned by him and completed by others. He was also responsible for the design of a lantern tower (a tower with high-up windows to let in light) for the cathedral.

Characteristically, Leonardo's architectural ideas were always innovative. His notebooks are full of plans for villas, castles, churches, stables and so on, but few, if any, ever got past the planning stage and there are no remaining buildings attributable to him. He saw buildings as being like living creatures, which could be ill and need the attention of a doctor/

architect. This tied in with the popular Renaissance idea of perfect structure and harmony within all forms – which included the human body, the buildings that man created, and ultimately the universe itself.

LEONARDO THE MUSICIAN

Leonardo was a highly skilled musician, not only in playing the lyre but also in inventing new musical instruments and special effects for theatre and pageants. His fame in this skill spread from Milan to other places as far away as France. The notebooks show designs for drums, wind instruments such as flutes and bagpipes, keyboards and organs. There are also way-out instruments, such as a lyre made from a weird beast's head, which was presumably related to the horse's head lyre that he brought to Milan.

Leonardo is known to have composed music as well, but sadly there are no known complete scores remaining, only little snatches. Often these are part of a riddle or a pun and accompanied by tiny drawings that relate to the tune or its lyrics. Above all harmony was important to Leonardo, not only in music and in natural sounds like that of running water, but in his paintings as well. He saw music in a mystical way, remarking that it represented invisible things. But for him painting was the supreme art because it endured, whereas music died as soon as it was created. How he would have loved to be let loose in a recording studio!

A portrait still exists that Leonardo must have painted in Milan, which shows how well he understood the soul of music. This is the *Portrait of a Musician* (c. 1485–90, (Pinacoteca Ambrosiana, Milan)). The musician is shown, score in hand, poised in a moment of profound stillness as if a piece of music is about to begin, possibly conducted by him.

LEONARDO THE PAINTER

Several other portraits exist which are partly or wholly attributable to Leonardo and it was undoubtedly an art form from which he obtained some of his living. Of these one of the finest has to be that of *Cecilia Gallerani* (c. 1483–88, Czartoryski Museum, Cracow, Poland.) This young lady is shown holding an ermine (a stoat in its white winter fur), probably a pun on her name from the Greek 'gale' for ermine. Cecilia has a delightful, lively, intelligent expression with more than a hint of mischief. Her pointed face and look of alert concentration are echoed by the lithe, wriggling ermine that she holds in her arms. Cecilia was a poetess and was Ludovico Sforza's mistress from 1490 when she was 17 years old. This portrait is an example of Leonardo at his best and shows a clear advance from the earlier portrait of Ginevra de Benci.

The Virgin of the Rocks

Several versions remain of this rather strange painting. The first, now in the Louvre, Paris, was part of an altarpiece, and was created by Leonardo, two of his pupils, and a sculptor. It was commissioned in 1483 by the Convent of San Francesco Grande in Milan, and depicts an apocryphal meeting in the desert between the infant St John and the infant Jesus. The painting that was commissioned was quite unlike the end result and the commissioners kicked up a fuss. On top of that some of the artists involved asked for more money. It is interesting to note that Leonardo's contribution to the project was valued at 100 lire. Although it is difficult to make comparisons with modern currency, Leonardo does note that Salai's set of clothes cost him 4 lire, so it seems that he was not paid very much considering the length of time the project would have taken.

The picture shows the Virgin with her arm around John, who kneels with his hands in an attitude of prayer. He is looking towards Jesus whose hand is raised as if in blessing of John. Beside Jesus is the angel Uriel, who rather mysteriously points at John, but whose gaze is diverted away, out of the picture altogether. A good deal of interesting debate has arisen as a result of this strange little group of figures. For example, some authors have suggested that the angel's pointing gesture implies secret **hermetic** symbolism, possibly connected with a cult of St John. The background is dark, with the sfumato so characteristic of Leonardo giving it a dreamlike, mythical air, which suggests that the scene is meant to

KEYWORD

Hermetic, to do with alchemy and other secret practices.

represent a symbolic, rather than an actual, event.

The fuss surrounding this painting gave rise to a lengthy lawsuit. It is unclear exactly what the lawsuit was about, but whatever the explanation a second version of the painting eventually appeared, a product of Leonardo's workshop, made c. 1506–8. This version is less glowing and mysterious and the angel no longer points to the young St John. This second picture (National Gallery, London) must have been acceptable, because it remained at the convent until bought by an Englishman in 1785.

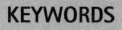

KEYWORDS

Mural, painting done directly onto a wall.

Lunette, half-moon shaped space above a door or window, often containing a painting or sculpture.

A secco, technique of painting on dry plaster.

The Last Supper (c. 1495–98)

This painting is a **mural**, commissioned by Ludovico and painted on a wall of the refectory of Santa Maria delle Grazie, a monastery in Milan. The scene shows Jesus sharing the last meal with his disciples before his crucifixion, and captures the moment when Jesus announces Judas's betrayal. Judas is shown having just upset the salt – traditionally a bad omen even today. Each disciple has a different expression, as if they have been caught in a freeze-frame. Their body language adds to the story too – one is speaking in his neighbour's ear, another points heavenwards with the mysterious pointing finger gesture that Leonardo so often used.

The painting is done in perspective to give an impression of looking through into another room, with a window at the far side. The disciples are all on one side of a long table, with Jesus seated in the middle. Above are three **lunettes**, showing the Sforza heraldic crests. The mural was done using an experimental technique with a combination of oils and varnish applied – a **secco**. This was horribly unsuccessful, for the underlying wall was damp and the masterpiece began to decay almost immediately: by 1556 it was reported by Vasari to be in a very poor state. Despite this problem the finished work won Leonardo international acclaim especially in France. Several attempts were made to transport the whole wall there – rumour has it that Napoleon was one of those to make the attempt – but happily it is still in its original position and even survived a bomb explosion in 1943. It has been painstakingly restored on various occasions.

Rumour has it that Napoleon attempted to take *The Last Supper* to France.

Most art critics look on this work as the climax of Leonardo's career as a painter. He spent many hours working on it and people reported that he often worked from dawn until dusk, never laying down his brush. Typically on other occasions he would come and have a look at the work, add a few touches and then wander off again. It was probably this unpredictable approach that infuriated Ludovico.

THE SFORZA MONUMENT

This flamboyant group project, commissioned by Ludovico and masterminded by Leonardo, was designed to bring prestige to all who were involved, but it turned out to be the ultimate failure. The idea was to build a colossal equestrian statue of cast bronze as a memorial to

Ludovico's father, Francesco Sforza, who had died in 1476. The idea was not new – there were earlier examples by both Verrocchio and Donatello – but this one was to beat them all by its sheer size. It was to be a staggering 7.2 metres height, twice the high of earlier statues, and therefore had to be designed to be moulded in separate sections.

Leonardo really took his time over this one, messing with it for many years. He did endless design sketches, including many fine anatomical sketches of horses and diagrams showing how the moulds were to be constructed. Some of these can still be seen in the Royal Library collection at Windsor, England. By December 1493 a full-scale clay model had been completed and was much admired. However, in 1494 fate stepped in as Charles VIII of France invaded Italy. The whole country was thrown into chaos as his troops swept through city after city. The 60 metric tons of bronze that had been set aside for the monument were sent by Ludovico to his father-in-law to be made into cannon, and the clay model was used mockingly for target practice by invading French troops. It was finally taken to the court of Ferrara, where it fell to bits. This seems very symbolic, for troubled times lay ahead, both for Italy and for Leonardo himself.

✳ ✳ ✳ ✳ SUMMARY ✳ ✳ ✳ ✳

● Leonardo spent nearly 20 years in Milan and produced some of his finest work while he was there, including *The Last Supper* and *The Virgin of the Rocks*.

● Milan was ruled by the Sforza family, whose head was Ludovico, 'Il Moro'. Milan's power arose mainly from military prowess but it was also an important commercial centre.

● Leonardo was a rather private person and did not bow easily to authority.

● While in Milan he worked as an engineer, mainly in hydraulics and the military field.

● He also attained international acclaim as a painter, musician, architect and inventor.

Troubled Times 1500-7

5

LEONARDO THE TRAVELLER

The destruction of his clay model for the Sforza horse probably served as a warning sign for Leonardo. He proceeded to set his financial affairs in order and then set off on a long journey through northern Italy, now ravaged by war. For companions he took with him Salai and his friend Luca Pacioli, who was one of the top mathematicians in Italy. Together they left Milan in December 1499. At the age of 47 Leonardo was about to begin the most unsettled phase of his whole life, where he travelled to many of the major cities in northern Italy and worked for various influential people.

During the plague years in Milan, Leonardo had occupied some of his time with a work of fiction, describing a fantastic and frightening journey over land and sea on a scientific mission for the Sultan of Egypt. He had probably talked to various interesting travellers both in Florence and Milan and had developed a fascination for tales of distant lands and for maps – he is said at one time to have owned a rare early map of the known world. The period from 1500 until 1507 gave him an opportunity to do more travelling himself – if not as far afield as he had been in his imagination – and he composed some very interesting maps of his own.

By now Leonardo was famous all over Italy both as a painter and a military engineer. He had no special loyalty or allegiance – his interest in politics was minimal and he simply worked for whoever made the best offers. First of all his party set off east for Mantua, where they were received by marchioness Isabella d'Este, the sister-in-law of Il Moro. She had already met Leonardo at Il Moro's court, and had become an admirer of his work. She had tried before to persuade him to do a portrait of her and during his brief stay in Mantua he did in fact produce one. This was a sketch, done in black lead and red chalk (now in the Louvre, Paris). This is an interesting drawing because it has been copied many times, first of all by Leonardo himself, using a special method of poking pinpricks around the outline of the profile through onto a second piece of paper. Leonardo promised Isabella that he would produce a full portrait in due course, but he never did and within two months he had left Mantua and was off on his travels again, this time to Venice.

Venice was at this time an influential and prosperous city and Pacioli had contacts there. It is possible that Leonardo went there in order to offer his skills as a military engineer, because a second invading army, not the French this time, but the Turkish Ottoman army, was threateningly camped a mere 50 kilometres away. The Ottoman presence was the result of a cunning ploy on the part of Il Moro. Venice had long been the enemy of the Sforzas, so Il Moro had persuaded the Turks to attack the Venetians to keep them busy while he was trying to get Milan back from the French.

While he was in Venice, Leonardo hatched various military schemes. The first one was to build a movable dam across the river Isonzo. This would build up a mass of water that could be used in a great tidal wave to wash away the threatening troops. The Venetian authorities rejected the idea, possibly because it was impractical. Undeterred Leonardo set about designing submarines to attack the Turkish ships underwater. Then he devised special diving suits and a primitive form of aqualung, which would allow divers to wreak unseen havoc below the water line. Leonardo had actually thought of this idea earlier, while he was still in Florence, but he had written a note to the effect that he would keep quiet about his invention, in case it fell into evil hands. It is not known whether he ever actually presented the idea to the authorities.

Meanwhile Il Moro's counter attack on Milan had failed. He was taken captive by the French and died in exile eight years later. Leonardo will no doubt have heard of the plight of his former patron, which effectively prevented his return to Milan. Venice did not hold him for long either and by April 1500 he was once more in Florence. He was based here on and off for the next seven years, with further periods of travel in between settled phases.

RETURN TO FLORENCE

Florence had changed greatly in the 20 years since Leonardo had been away. Verrocchio had died in 1488. Lorenzo the Magnificent had died too, in 1492, and Florence was no longer ruled by the Medici family. An opportunist Dominican monk called Savonarola had

KEYWORD

Iconoclastic, attacking popular beliefs and destroying religious imagery such as paintings.

proclaimed himself as a republican leader and under his influence there had been a brief period of social and moral austerity. His religion was strictly fundamentalist, of the fire and brimstone variety. He was an **iconoclastic** preacher and many works of art had perished as a result of his censorship. Various friends of Leonardo, such as Botticelli, were out of favour, denounced as being decadent. However, Pope Alexander VI soon saw Savonarola as a threat and had him excommunicated. He was hanged and burnt at the stake in 1497.

Leonardo had fortunately managed to miss all these upheavals and arrived back in Florence at the right time to enjoy a productive artistic period. He was already a popular artist and soon found himself accommodation at the expense of an order of Servite monks, who commissioned him to produce a painting of the Virgin and St Anne. This had originally been offered to another popular painter, Filippino Lippi (c. 1457–1504, son of Filippo Lippi), but he passed the commission on to Leonardo. The monks waited patiently, but Leonardo seemed to be much occupied with other projects.

His notebooks show that he was busy with experiments on topics such as acoustics and learning mathematical ideas from Pacioli. He became interested in the idea of human flight, studying the flight of birds and assuming that people would ultimately fly in the same way, by gliding and flapping huge wings. A notebook on the flight of birds, dated c. 1505, shows some of his recorded ideas about this. He also did some work as an architect, drawing up plans for villas and churches.

The monks waited patiently.

Meanwhile Isabella kept trying to get in touch from Mantua, hoping to get Leonardo to undertake various commissions, but he seems never to have bothered to reply. Quite likely funds were still fairly comfortable, for Il Moro had rewarded him handsomely during his last years in Milan. Much of the work that he produced during this period in Florence has been lost, and we know about it only because of preliminary sketches and subsequent copies by other artists. Some of the more famous examples are:

* *Neptune*. Vasari describes a picture, now lost, full of the movement and action typical of Leonardo – furious winds, boiling ocean waves, racing dolphins and Neptune's chariot drawn by plunging sea horses. A similar drawing is now in the collection at Windsor, England.

* *Madonna with the Yarn Winder*. This picture was based on an apocryphal story where the Virgin Mary was supposed to have spun

purple cloth for the temple, using a yarn winder shaped like a cross. The symbolic implication is that she is spinning the future – the thread representing destiny and the yarn winder the cross. Various versions of this picture from Leonardo's workshop still exist.

* *Leda and the Swan.* Various copies remain of this painting, but the original was lost in the seventeenth century. The picture depicts a scene from classical myth, where Leda, who represents a Mother Nature archetype, is seduced by Zeus, the father of the gods, in the form of a swan. She produces two swans' eggs, from which hatch two sets of twins. Leda has the intricately coiled and plaited hair and demure expression so often painted by Leonardo. The details of the painting are also classic Leonardo: the background shows a dramatic landscape in muted colours and in the foreground are many detailed flowers and shrubs. Various sketches for this painting have survived, including ones of Leda's head in various positions and little botanical sketches, dated between 1504 and 1513.

At last, Leonardo deigned to produce a **cartoon** for the painting that the monks had commissioned. This cartoon *Virgin and Child with St Anne* (National Gallery, London) is one of his most famous surviving works. According to Vasari the cartoon was an instant

> **KEYWORD**
>
> Cartoon, full-sized drawing as a preliminary for a painting.

hit and for two days people of all kinds crowded into Leonardo's workshop to gaze at it in awe. The picture shows the infant Jesus blessing the infant St John, and St Anne making the famous upward pointing gesture. It is certainly a lovely work of art, with the characteristic Leonardo drapery and the gently smiling faces of the two women, who look as if they are sharing some mysterious secret.

Leonardo did start the painting but although he worked on it sporadically until 1508, once again he seems to have failed to deliver the finished masterpiece to the commissioners. He reworked the theme at various times until the end of his life and a painting of it is in the Louvre, Paris, dated c. 1508–18. This version, which is probably not all by Leonardo's own hand, omits the infant John and shows Jesus with a lamb. Meanwhile Leonardo received a more exciting offer that he could not refuse – to work as a military engineer for the notorious Cesare Borgia.

TRAVELS WITH CESARE BORGIA

Cesare Borgia has earned a place in history as a ruthless despot and he was certainly a nasty piece of work, murdering anybody, including relations, who stood in his way. The people of Florence were his enemies and strugged to keep free of his dictatorship. Born in 1475 he was an illegitimate son of Pope Alexander VI. His sister Lucrezia was equally unpleasant, and they are rumoured to have enjoyed an incestuous relationship. Cesare, whose motto was 'Aut Cesare aut nihil' ('Caesar or nothing'), was a famous adventurer and had a rather dashing reputation which may have seemed extremely attractive at the time. He was a successful soldier and had a burning ambition to conquer the whole of Italy, so he was in need of a clever military engineer.

Leonardo kept a tiny notebook, about 11 × 7 cm, now known as *Manuscript L*, which gives us a first-hand account of the nine months or so that he spent travelling through northern and central Italy as Borgia's engineer. He went from city to city, advising about better defence systems and fortifications such as walls, bridges and buttresses. His notes are full of ideas for fantastic underground tunnels, secret hidden chambers and machines of war. Firearms were new at this time and were revolutionizing warfare. Leonardo was not slow to design new varieties, such as a ten-barrelled canon that would function not unlike a modern machine gun. He also experimented with ways of increasing the range of existing weapons, particularly crossbows, and improving loading and firing methods. He even invented a kind of 'tank', consisting of a cone-shaped shell with guns sticking out around the bottom of it. Inside, toothed wheels and cranks allowed the tank to be steered in any direction.

During his travels Leonardo met various influential people such as Niccolo Machiavelli, who was working as an envoy and spy for Borgia.

This encounter was clearly a meeting of two great minds, which led to a close friendship. Leonardo was well paid by Borgia and not directly involved in any warfare himself, but by about October 1502 he had quit the job. This is most likely because he could not cope with various atrocities committed by Borgia. For example, a group of men whose leader was called Vitelli, whom Leonardo knew personally, had rebelled against Borgia. Borgia had pretended to forgive them and had then had them all murdered when he was supposed to be discussing reconciliation terms. Whatever the reason, by March 1503 Leonardo was once more in Florence, again demonstrating that he would side with whoever happened to suit his needs at the time. Cesare Borgia's empire soon collapsed and he died in 1507.

LEONARDO THE CARTOGRAPHER

During his spell in Florence and while on his travels with Cesare Borgia, Leonardo drew all kinds of maps which show that he had

KEYWORD

Cartography, map-making.

astounding skill in **cartography**. He drew physical maps of Tuscany, Emilia and Romagna, which cover surprisingly large areas, displaying all the fine details of mountains, blue swirling rivers and lakes, and showing contours with different shades of brown. It is difficult to see how he achieved these unless he had a colossal team of surveyors at work, or managed to get one of his amazing flying machines airborne! He also drew town maps, such as a map of Imola, which is again very detailed, showing all the roads.

While Leonardo was busy with Cesare Borgia, Pisa, formerly a dependent of Florence, declared independence. Florence promptly laid siege to the town and a stalemate situation developed that went on for months. Leonardo went to the area and drew some maps showing a plan that he had devised with Machiavelli to divert the river Arno, thus depriving Pisa of its water supply. This plan was actually put into action by the Florentine authorities, and although it failed it paved the way for a peaceful settlement of the dilemma. Three maps still survive showing details of the scheme. Leonardo had actually had plans for many years that involved changing the course of the river Arno in order to supply more towns with water and improve irrigation and navigation. He envisaged a sort of industrial corridor between Pisa and Florence with mills along the river powering industries such as pottery and paper-making. He also dreamed up a series of locks on the tributaries to the river, thus making them more navigable for trading.

THE BATTLE OF ANGHIARI

On 24 October 1503 Leonardo was given an important commission to paint a huge mural on the wall of the council chamber in the Palazzo del Signoria in Florence. On the strength of this commission he was given a studio and accommodation in the Hall of the Pope at Santa Maria Novella, which was both a church and a hospital. The Signoria (government officials) chose a triumphant battle scene for the mural, showing the victory of Florence over Milan in 1440 at Anghiari. After his work as a military engineer Leonardo was the perfect man for the job.

However, there was a major snag. Leonardo's arch-rival Michelangelo had been commissioned to paint another battle scene on the opposite wall of the same room. The two men disliked one another, probably because they were opposites in many ways as well as being in com-petition. Michelangelo was from a well-off family and had had a good education – just the sort to irritate Leonardo. Not only that, he was a religious fanatic too, whereas Leonardo's views on the Church were notoriously unorthodox. Both men were artists of great genius, but it seems they could not exchange a civil word. The ensuing rivalry, aptly nicknamed the 'Battle of Battles', kept Leonardo hard at it for once and fascinated crowds gathered to watch as he spent ages preparing a detailed cartoon for the mural.

Meanwhile Leonardo was still busy with his other interests as usual. His notebooks show lots of interesting mechanical devices, mathematical conundrums, and his ideas about flight. He had various ongoing personal problems as well – his father died, and he also had to go to

The Battle of Battles.

Milan for a court case involving the *Virgin of the Rocks*. However, at last the cartoon was finished and it was taken across to the council chamber where the scaffolding was ready for Leonardo to begin painting the mural. But the project was fraught with difficulty from the first day. He was just about to pick up his brush 6 on June 1505 when it suddenly grew dark and began pouring with rain. Somehow the cartoon got soaked and began to come apart. This was only the beginning of the problems – it turned out that the linseed oil that had been provided was of poor quality so the paint did not mix well. The paint ran, and the plaster began to crumble off the wall.

As if that were not enough, Leonardo was getting involved in yet another dispute. He had obtained a contract from Louis XII, King of France, to do some paintings and Louis now began to make it clear that Leonardo's presence was required in Milan. A dispute arose between the Signoria of Florence and Louis and for a while Leonardo commuted between Florence and Milan. A small finished section of the mural survived for a while, but in the end both this and the cartoon perished. All we have left now are various sketches of bits of the battle such as rearing horses and anguished soldiers' faces caught almost as though by a camera. Michelangelo never finished his mural either – in fact he did not even begin it, because he was summoned to Rome by Pope Julius II to paint the ceiling of the Sistine Chapel. One can imagine that the Signoria were not amused.

In March 1507, Leonardo's beloved Uncle Francesco died, naming Leonardo as his sole heir. This gave rise to yet another court case when Leonardo's half-brothers decided to contest the will. By the spring of 1508, Leonardo left Florence for Milan. Once again Florence seemed to have brought him a lot of headaches.

❋ ❋ ❋ ❋ SUMMARY ❋ ❋ ❋ ❋

● After leaving Milan, Leonardo was based mainly in Florence for the next seven years.

● He also travelled extensively through northern and central Italy on various commissions, including a few months as military engineer to Cesare Borgia.

● Leonardo was very productive during this period in Florence, but once again he failed to complete important commissions.

● His notebooks show that he was interested in and working on many projects as well as his work as an artist.

● Although it was in many ways one of his most important commissions, his mural of the Battle of Anghiari was never finished.

Leonardo's Notebooks 1

6

THE JOTTINGS OF A GENIUS

Leonardo seems to have been a great scribbler of notes and a collector of interesting ideas right from his early days at Verrocchio's workshop. More systematic note-keeping emerged when he was about 30, during his time in Milan. From this time onwards he tended to carry a notebook around with him so that he could jot down anything of interest. It is sometimes possible to date these notes approximately according to the content – for example in the 1490s there are notes about theatrical ideas for the Sforza court and by about 1496, after he met Pacioli, mathematical ideas and geometrical designs begin to appear.

Leonardo's jottings were chaotic in the sense that his mind was constantly full of all sorts of ideas at once. The sheets of paper are full of scientific observations, comments about art, little jokes and puns, sketches of the world around him, philosophical notions and shopping lists, all apparently muddled up. And yet the striking thing about these little pages is the incredible neatness of the writing and the economy with paper – every corner is used. Strangely, most of the notes are written backwards, starting on the right-hand side of the page and flowing neatly across the page in perfect mirror writing. There has been a lot of speculation as to the reason for this oddity and it has added to the general mystique of Leonardo. He was left-handed, so it may be that he simply found it more natural to write this way – a habit that persisted uncorrected from childhood. Other people claim that he did it in order to conceal what he wrote, possibly to avoid claims of plagiarism or to keep his inventions secret. Some of his later notes are encoded as well as being written in mirror writing. Leonardo did in fact use normal writing, or employed a scribe, when he needed others to read his work. It is possible that in his own notebooks he simply didn't make the effort and was just keen to get the ideas down on paper as his brain raced ahead. Interestingly he is reported to have used both hands when drawing and painting.

About five years after he settled in Milan, Leonardo decided to be more systematic with his jottings and he began to plan a series of treatises on various topics, such as flight. Characteristically he never really got his act together on this and for the main part his notes remained fragmented. After his death he left all his notes, by now a huge collection of sheets of paper and little notebooks, to his friend and pupil Francesco Melzi. Happily a lot of this material has survived. One of the most important collections forms a big scrapbook of 4,000 or so sheets, now known as the *Codex Atlanticus* (Ambrosiana Library, Milan). This provides a great deal of the information we have about Leonardo apart from biographical sources. A further 13 manuscripts, labelled A–M, are in the library of the Institute de France, Paris. Three more notebooks are in the Victoria and Albert Museum, London and there is a fine collection of drawings at Windsor Castle, England. Still more manuscripts are widely scattered, in London, Turin and other cities, as well as in private collections. (See Further Reading for more information.)

THE ORGANIZED COSMOS

Leonardo viewed the world in an unusual way because he was both scientist and artist. He always stressed the importance of careful observation of nature and was critical of learning gained only from books and words. For him the universe itself was an organized whole, rather like a work of art, and he saw this structure reflected in miniature throughout the natural world. For example, during his time in Milan he developed ideas about linking architecture with the proportions of the human body. When his friend Pacioli wrote a treatise called 'De Divina Proportione', Leonardo provided a sketch for the frontispiece showing how the human body with arms and legs outstretched would fit into a circle or a square. This curious little figure with four arms and four legs is so famous today that it is almost a Leonardo logo.

This kind of idea was not new, but came from a Roman architect called Vitruvius, and also from Euclid, the Greek mathematician. The human figure was a reflection of the cosmos, with its navel, in the centre of the

Leonardo always stressed the importance of careful observation of nature.

circle, corresponding to the **omphalos**. Pacioli taught Leonardo a great deal of Euclidian geometry. Leonardo was very excited by this and produced lots of drawings of complex **polyhedra**, some of which were used to illustrate Pacioli's work.

KEYWORDS

Omphalos, the centre or hub of something.

Polyhedra, solid figures, such as cubes, with many faces.

Leonardo's ideas about scientific thinking were similar in many ways to modern methods:

* He always began by observing the natural world, using the five senses.

* Next he tried to arrive at general laws, based upon these observations.

* He tried always to proceed step by step, in a methodical way.

* He tested his ideas by means of experiments.

He tried to use this method of thinking both in his work as a scientist and engineer and as an artist. His ideas were not all original – he relied on studies of ancient and medieval scholars and the exchange of ideas with people that he met. By about 1495 he had made lots of notes on a vast range of topics, and had also collected a library of his own, which contained about 40 books. But he often carried his thinking far ahead of others, particularly in the fields of technology, with his many marvellous inventions, and in optics and anatomy (see Chapter 7).

In Leonardo's time, the universe was usually seen as being a vast sphere, created by God and containing the four elements – earth, air, fire and water – arranged in concentric regions which constantly got mixed up and kept rearranging themselves. Leonardo more or less accepted this idea, but gradually modified it through his own observations. For example, he questioned the contemporary idea that sea shells found high up in the mountains had been carried there by the biblical flood, or else had simply somehow grown inside the rocks. After careful observations he decided that both ideas were nonsense and that the shells must have got there long ago, before the mountains were raised – a conclusion remarkably similar to that of modern science.

Leonardo was particularly interested in the effects of water and weathering. He saw water as being the most important agent in the formation of the earth's structure and mentioned that floods were the most powerful natural threat to human property. In one of his notebooks he makes a whole list of topics about water, such as 'Different depths of rivers', 'Currents on the surfaces of water' and 'Shapes of hills uncovered by water'. This kind of planning occurs at intervals throughout the notebooks, indicating that Leonardo was intending to undertake more systematic studies, but never got round to it. He was also fascinated by astronomy, erecting a primitive observatory by placing an optical instrument of his own making under a skylight in his roof in order to observe the moon. He made a startling but brief observation that 'the sun does not move' more than a hundred years before the scientist Galileo got into deep trouble with the Church for saying the same thing.

Leonardo developed his own ideas about four 'powers', namely motion, weight, force and percussion, that represented the key to the way in which the universe worked. He planned a book on theoretical mechanics and made further long lists about the effects of force and movement. He was interested in these ideas chiefly because they were important to him in his work as military engineer and inventor. Once again he constantly questioned accepted theories and developed his own. For example, he contested the accepted theory about the flight of an arrow. The current theory was that the arrow sent out a sort of bow wave, which prevented its flight from being hindered. Leonardo disagreed with this, saying that the air passing in waves in front of the arrow actually slowed down its flight. Time and again it is clear from his notebooks that Leonardo had a highly original way of thinking that made him into a great inventor.

AMAZING MACHINES

A stroll round a collection of reconstructed inventions from Leonardo's notebooks, such as that in the museum in Vinci today, soon gives you a very good idea why he hardly ever finished any paintings. He was fascinated by the way things worked and seems to have invented just about everything! The possibility of perpetual motion interested him, again reflecting the idea of perfection that so fascinated Renaissance thinkers. He wanted to develop technology as far as possible and to save time and effort by means of better machines. In this way his thinking was in line with modern technological ideas such as automation and robotics. Very often he would examine a contemporary machine and then set about finding ways of improving it. His notebooks contain numerous meticulous exploded drawings showing all the intricate workings of many different kinds of clocks, looms, mills, presses and other machines.

Machines for construction work

Leonardo was not the first to draw machines to be used in building construction. Brunelleschi invented and drew many new ideas such as a whole series of winches and cranes when he was working on the construction of the cupola for Florence Cathedral. He was a talented engineer and devised schemes for diverting rivers as well as an interesting 'chariot that flies in water' – a device for transporting marble to Florence, that apparently got disastrously stuck in the river Arno. Leonardo copied Brunelleschi's ideas and then modified them and added new ones of his own. For example, he designed a crane to raise rocks vertically through space, and a winch that would hoist a load and then move it horizontally. He also devised a complicated hammer winch that dropped three trip hammers in turn onto pegs sticking out of a large cylinder, so making the cylinder turn.

Clocks

Leonardo made many pages of notes about clocks of various sorts, such as a highly ingenious one that showed not only the hours but also the phases of the moon and the astrological houses. He even invented a special stabilizer for large clocks, which would ensure that the power supplied by the spring mechanism would remain constant.

Looms and printing presses

Mechanical looms and printing presses were new in Leonardo's day and again he played around with new designs and improvements. For example, he devised a machine that would twist thread and wind it onto a bobbin ready for the loom. Both looms and printing presses incorporated the idea of automation that fascinated Leonardo.

Machines for everyday life

Many of Leonardo's ideas were designed to make life easier for ordinary people. For example, he made a design for a vertical worm-screw press for crushing olives and collecting the oil. This was probably a refinement of the olive press that was in use at Anchiano where he was born, traces of which can still be seen. He designed an automatic saw, a hole-boring machine with an automatic centring device and a special grindstone with a built-in sieve. More specialized machines included a mirror polishing machine and a rolling mill that was designed to produce sheets of tin 30 cm wide. All these and many more fascinating ideas appear in the pages of his notebooks.

Travel over land and water

One of Leonardo's most famous inventions is a spring driven 'car'. Actually the idea is sketchy – the complex propulsion mechanism was never completed, but the basics are there, including a steering shaft, and the car has definitely captured people's imagination. Related to this was a crank-operated cart, with a front steering lever. He also drew a paddleboat with blades moved by means of large man-operated cranks, and an idea for floats like huge skis that enabled a man to walk on water. Safety was even taken into consideration when he supplied a lifebuoy in a ring shape, much like the modern life-preserver.

The most amazing transport idea of them all presents us with an intriguing mystery. This is Leonardo's bicycle, which only came to light fairly recently when parts of the *Codex Atlanticus* were being restored. A picture showing a perfect bicycle complete with pedals, saddle, handlebars and chain, appeared when two sheets of paper that had been pasted together at the end of the sixteenth century were peeled apart. Curiously the picture does not appear to have been drawn by Leonardo himself – the only word on the page is 'Salai', which suggests that the mischievous pupil was copying an idea of his master. The rest of the page is devoted to rather badly drawn obscene sketches.

FLIGHT

Leonardo was interested in birds and the ways in which they flew all his life. He spent many years studying them, as well as bats and insects such as butterflies and dragonflies. He observed how kites and eagles soared high up into the sky by striking their wings against the air, and compared this with the way in which the wind fills a ship's sails and moves the vessel along. Amazingly he concluded that an object in the air exerts the same amount of pressure against the air as the air exerts against the object – thus beating Newton to this theory by 200 years. His prediction was that if a man had wings big enough and attached in the right way he could actually overcome the resistance of the air. Leonardo also carefully observed the way birds could hover in the air by making balancing movements with wings and tail.

Leonardo saw the achievement of flight as being almost a divine calling for an engineer, because it represented the farthest limits to which human beings could aspire. The Greek myth of Daedalus and Icarus fascinated him and references to it keep cropping up in the notebooks. Daedalus was an inventor who made wings out of wax and feathers for his son Icarus and himself. Icarus flew so close to the sun that his wings melted and he came to a sad end. Man had long dreamed of flight and to master it would certainly have been the ultimate achievement for Leonardo.

Leonardo's own ideas for take-off are very inventive. He began with flying machines based on bird's wings that flapped in order to get airborne. One of these has an automatic return mechanism to bring the wings back to their original position. Another is designed to rest on the aviator's shoulders and the flapping movement is achieved by raising and lowering the feet. A lever for steering via a rudder goes around the person's neck. Leonardo also designed instruments to go inside the flying machine, such as a primitive inclinometer, made from a plumb line housed in a transparent cone to protect it from the wind. There was even an anemometer for measuring the force of the wind before take off. This was based on a hinged vane attached to a quadrant scale, very similar to modern instruments.

Leonardo also designed gliders and a sort of helicopter, comprising of a spiral of linen twisted around a vertical shaft. He may have got the idea for this by observing things such as windmills and winged seeds. He also invented a parachute, a full-scale version of which was recently built and tested by skydiver Adrian Nicholas. Despite the fact that the parachute was made of wood and canvas and had no hole for air to escape at the top, it worked perfectly on a trial drop from a hot air balloon at 10,000 feet.

STORIES AND REFLECTIONS
Leonardo's notebooks are full of interesting little tales, riddles and words of wisdom. Many of these will have been collected for use at

social and court gatherings in his role as entertainer. He had in his library books which he used as source material, such as:

* *Aesop's Fables.* Aesop was a Greek storyteller, who was supposedly a slave.

* *Pliny's Natural History.* Pliny (c. AD 23–79) was a Roman polymath, who wrote books about botany, geography, zoology, life and the universe.

* Medieval **bestiaries** such as the popular *Flowers of Virtue.*

Leonardo also invented many stories, jokes, fables and words of wisdom of his own. These tell us a great deal about Leonardo's outlook on life as well as the times he lived in.

Stories taken from the bestiaries

These are usually very short and contain a moral lesson. This lesson will either expose a vice such as avarice, envy or sloth, or else extol a virtue such as patience or humility. For example:

* *The oyster – treachery.* When the moon is full the oyster opens its shell wide. The crafty crab throws in a piece of seaweed or a stone to jam the shell open so that it can eat the oyster. It is the same with a person who opens his mouth to let out a secret and lays himself wide open to interested gossips.

* *The mole – lies.* The mole has very small eyes and lives always underground in the dark. If it comes up into the light it dies straightaway because it becomes known. It is the same with lies.

Leonardo's own fables

Leonardo made up many little fables of his own, based on life in the countryside where he grew up. These are particularly fascinating because so little has changed since Leonardo's time – the olives, vines and figs, the ants, spiders and blackbirds are still there, going about their daily business just as he describes. Leonardo often missed the quiet fields of his boyhood when he went to live in the city and he gradually developed a very jaundiced view of urban life. This is poignantly shown in the first of the following tales:

* *The stone by the roadside – love for solitude and country life.* A stone lived on the edge of a lovely grove full of plants and flowers. But below was a road, where it could see many other stones, and so, feeling lonely, it let itself slide down onto the road. It soon regretted this, however, because it was constantly run over by carts, trodden on and getting covered in dung. In vain it looked up at the tranquil place it had come from. So it is with people who leave a life of quiet contemplation and go to live in the city, among people of infinite evil.

* *The citron (lemon) – consequences of pride and haughtiness.* The citron thought itself so beautiful that it set itself apart from other trees and so, losing their sheltering protection, was uprooted by the wind.

Words of wisdom
Most of Leonardo's words of wisdom are comments based upon ordinary, everyday aspects of human life. Again we can see his rather despairing attitude towards the vices of his fellow men. In particular he saw the struggle against poverty and the greed for money as basic social evils.

* *Of money and gold* – These will come out of great pits in the ground and will make people toil endlessly with great anguish in order to gain them.

* *Of the cruelty of men* – Creatures will be seen on the earth who are always fighting one another with great malice and cruelty. They will cut down many forests, and even when they are full of food they will carry on destroying things for pleasure. 'Nothing shall remain on the earth, or under the earth, or in the waters that shall not be pursued, disturbed or spoiled.' (A chilling warning for our times – for the full quote see *The Notebooks of Leonardo* – details in Further Reading.)

Jests

These tend to be rather long and contrived for modern taste, but they show Leonardo's sense of humour. Perhaps the second example was based on a real-life incident?

* *The miller and the ass* – Two men were arguing about reincarnation. One of them tried to prove his point by saying that he remembered the other had been a miller. Whereupon the second replied that it was all coming back to him – the first man had been the ass who had carried his sacks of flour.

* *The priest and the artist* – It was Easter Saturday and the priest came into the artist's studio and ruined half his paintings by sprinkling holy water on them. When challenged he replied that he was only doing his duty, and as such expected to be rewarded a hundredfold from on high. When he stepped outside the artist threw a bucket of water all over him from an upstairs window.

Reflections

Little reflections upon life were slipped in at random among other notes in Leonardo's notebooks. For example:

* 'What is fair in men passes and does not last.'

* 'When fortune comes, seize her in front with a sure hand, because behind she is bald.'

* 'Just as iron rusts from disuse, and stagnant water putrefies, or when cold turns to ice, so our intellect wastes unless it is kept in use.'

* 'A body may sooner be without its shadow than virtue without envy.'

* And finally, the delightfully poetic line – 'He turns not back who is bound to a star.'

(All quoted from *The Notebooks of Leonardo da Vinci*.)

✳ ✳ ✳ ✳ *SUMMARY* ✳ ✳ ✳ ✳

- Leonardo had a tendency throughout life to jot down ideas on pieces of paper.

- From about age 30 onwards he tended to be a little more systematic about his jottings, and often carried a notebook around with him.

- His notebooks are full of an amazing diversity of facts, sketches, jokes, little snatches of music, inventions, shopping lists, stories and reflections on life.

- He was always alert for new ideas and developed many of his amazing machines and words of wisdom by building upon the work of others.

- His intention to organize his notebooks into proper treatises on different subjects was never carried out.

7

Leonardo's Notebooks II

THE ARTS

Leonardo's notes about art and painting are scattered widely throughout all his other notes and are no more systematic than the rest. In the middle of the sixteenth century a lot of

KEYWORD

Transcript, written copy.

material was gathered up into a **transcript** known as the 'Trattato della Pittura' ('Treatise on painting'), now in the Vatican Library, Rome. This contains writing about the life of an artist, the nature of art and the scientific aspects of painting. There were various copies made and much of the original writing has now been lost, but the Treatise is valuable because it gives us insight into Leonardo's personal views. He probably did in fact finish other works on the subject – for example Pacioli wrote in 1498 that Leonardo had finished a book on 'depiction and movements of men', but this has also been lost.

Leonardo saw painting as the most important of the art forms, ranking it above music and poetry, and seeing the painter as 'lord of all types of people'. He compared the poet's representation of the human figure with that of the artist, saying that the poet's version was dismembered, whereas the artist's was whole. Sculpture too was a lesser art, requiring less thought and skill than painting, because it simply shows us the shape of things and no more (possibly this remark was a dig at Michelangelo!). He emphasized the importance for the artist of study-ing natural science and mathematics, because painting was a way of representing nature. Two fields of scientific study – anatomy and optics – were of special interest to him. The eye was for him 'the window of the soul', which gives us our understanding of the infinite works of nature.

Leonardo gives a lot of advice to the young artist and his ideas give us insight into his own personality. He advises the artist to spend a lot of time alone in order to focus his thoughts and to live in small rooms because large spaces distract the mind. On the other hand, he also advises the student to spend time drawing in company, because the competitive element will spur him to greater effort and the exchange of ideas is important. While out walking in the country he should closely observe natural things and take notes – Leonardo suggests carrying a notebook around all the time, just as he did himself. Among his fellow men the student should always be alert to gesture and facial expression.

The student should always be alert to gesture and facial expression.

Winter evenings are spent working on things that were prepared during the summer – we must remember of course that there was no electric light in Leonardo's day, and useful daylight would be limited in the winter time. Leonardo emphasizes that the artist should not work for the sake of riches, but rather in order to gain renown in his field. He should always work slowly, basing his work on sound theory and close observation.

OBSERVING THE NATURAL WORLD

Geometry

An understanding of geometry is important to the painter because he is trying to represent solid objects on a flat surface. Leonardo records ideas about points, lines, surfaces and solid geometrical shapes such as pyramids, in order to explain how the artist can build up an illusion of 3D in a painting. On the other hand he warns that geometry and arithmetic both reduce things down to their component parts and therefore neither can fully express the wholeness of the natural world.

Light, shade and colour

Study of the effects of light and shadow are of paramount importance to the artist. Leonardo gives careful discussions about this, including little diagrams showing how objects cast shadows. He says that shadows are essential in creating effects of perspective, because without them opaque and solid bodies are ill defined. Every opaque body is surrounded by shadow, and its surface is enveloped in shadow and light. The painter should make the shadow darkest when close to an object and then gradually fade it away to infinity. The more brilliant the light of a luminous body, the darker should be the accompanying shadows.

Leonardo makes a lot of comments about light and shadow and obviously observed their effects carefully in the world around him, always seeing things with an artist's eye. For example, he remarks that 'very great charm of shadow and light is to be found in the faces of those who sit in the doors of dark houses'. He observes different types of illumination – those from direct sources such as the sun or a candle, as compared with diffuse light on cloudy or misty days, and subdued light such as twilight. Colours vary according to the amount of light – in a luminous space they reveal greater beauty and in shadow they are muted. Leonardo identifies six 'simple' colours, from which all others are mixed. These are white, yellow, green, blue, red and black. He explains at length how to use colours next to one another in order to obtain different forms of contrast. Changes of colour produced by the effect of atmosphere intervening between object and eye can be used to build up the sense of perspective. 'The art of painting', he says, 'shows by means of its science, wide landscapes with distant horizons on a flat surface.'

There are some delightful comments about the colours of trees, for example: 'The accidental colours of the leaves of trees are four, namely shadow, light, lustre and transparency' and '…if you are on the side whence the wind is blowing you will see the trees looking much lighter than you would see them on the other sides; and this is due to the fact that the wind turns up the reverse side of the leaves which in all trees is much whiter than the upper side.' It is clear that much of Leonardo's talent stemmed from his extraordinary gift for minute observation of everyday things that most of us would pass by.

Botany

There are many notes about different aspects of landscape, such as the movement and forms of clouds and water and the formation of rocks. Botany in particular is an important study for the artist because plants and trees are so often used in painting backgrounds. Numerous drawings of plants native to Italy are scattered through Leonardo's notebooks and he was fascinated by the scientific study of their lives. He carefully studied topics such as plant growth, the effects of gravity and sunlight, the development of rings in tree trunks, the flow of sap and the arrangement of leaves. He not only observed the plants in the natural world, he also did experiments, such as one where he left a gourd with only one small root and then watered it until it produced abundant fruit. The infinite variety of nature was a delight to him: '…among trees of the same kind there would not be found one which nearly resembles another, and not only the plants as a whole, but among their branches, leaves and fruit, will not be found one which is precisely like another.'

Proportion

As we have already seen, proportion and harmony in painting, sculpture and architecture were very important during the Renaissance and reflected the perfection of the cosmos. Leonardo wrote many notes, accompanied by diagrams, about the importance of using correct proportion in order to obtain harmony in painting. For example: 'From the roots of the hair to the bottom of the chin is the tenth part of a man's height…from the nipples to the crown of the head is a fourth part of the man…' and so on. He also made remarks about human growth, such as: 'Every man at three years is half the full height he will grow to at last.' He compares the effect of a harmonious painting to a beautiful piece of music, saying that 'the effect of an angelic face in painting is much greater, for those proportions produce a harmonious concord which reaches the eye simultaneously, just as a chord of music affects the ear'.

Movement of the body

Leonardo explains how to make human figures come alive and appear to have grace and movement rather than standing stiffly and woodenly. Again his notes are accompanied by little diagrams, such as one of a man walking upstairs and another of a man getting up off the ground. Observations are carefully made from life in a scientific manner, for example: 'The sinew which guides the leg, and which is connected with the patella of the knee, feels it a greater labour to carry the man upwards in proportion as the leg is more bent.' He emphasizes that the movements of the human body, like other things in nature, are infinitely varied. In painting, the limbs are especially important and should be shown in natural, dynamic positions, with joints bent.

Draperies

Leonardo says that drapery and garments are important in painting because they show a lot about the person who is wearing them – for example they can indicate the rank of the wearer. Different qualities of cloth lie differently and show different types of folds. The play of light, showing folds and shadows, is very important to make the drapery look natural, and suggestions of fluttering can indicate movement of the wearer, or the action of the wind. If a person is wearing a cloak, the shape of the underlying figure should not be too clear – there must be a suggestion of other garments underneath the cloak. On the other hand nymphs and angels are portrayed in light, flowing garments that are pressed against the body by the flowing of the wind and so suggest a more ethereal, spiritual nature.

Expression of the spirit

Leonardo considered the highest purpose of the artist to be the expression of the spirit within the body. Accurate anatomical observation is not enough, and the artist must penetrate deeper. Faces and gestures must reveal the inner frame of mind and personality and hands and arms must display the intentions of the mind that is moving them. 'A good painter has two chief objects to paint, man and the intention of his soul; the former is easy, the latter hard, because he has to represent it by the attitudes and movements of the limbs.' Interestingly Leonardo suggests learning about body language by observing dumb people, because he says that their actions are more natural than those of other people.

Different types of people should be represented in different ways. For example old men should be shown with slow and heavy movements, their legs bent at the knee and the head leaning forwards. Women are shown in modest attitudes, with legs close together, arms folded, and heads inclined. Old women on the other hand are shown with 'eager, swift and furious gestures, like infernal furies'! Little children show lively wriggling movements when sitting and shy attitudes when standing.

OPTICS AND PERSPECTIVE

Leonardo's ideas about perception belong to his own age, in that he believed that the five senses – touch, sight, smell, taste and hearing – feed information into an 'organ of perception' which in turn activates 'the sensus communis'. This rather vague organ, which roughly corresponded to the soul, was supposed to be located in the centre of the brain, and Leonardo set about trying to find it. The concept is not too far removed from modern theories about incoming sensory information stimulating the brain. The organ that interested Leonardo above all others was the eye, 'the window of the soul', and he saw it as being superior to all the other organs. He stressed that the painter must analyze information coming from the eye in order to make his painting like a window looking out into a section of the visible world.

Leonardo saw perspective as 'the bridle and rudder of painting'. He identified three aspects of perspective that the painter should be aware of:

* Objects appear smaller the further away they are.
* Colours vary according to distance.
* Objects further away appear less distinct.

He records a whole list of perspective effects for the attention of the artist, and includes diagrams to illustrate particular points. A manuscript dated 1508–9 names ten different attributes of vision that the painter needs to study: darkness/brightness, substance, colour, form, place, remoteness/nearness and movement/rest.

During his time in Milan, Leonardo began a notebook dedicated to the study of light, shade and optical devices. Building on his experiences from the artist's point of view, he began to approach the subject in a more scientific way, formulating theories and developing new optical devices. He studied earlier work such as that by Greek physician Galen, and other scientists and philosophers including contemporary thinkers. He also performed dissections on animal and human eyes. Gradually Leonardo became a pioneer in the study of optics, years ahead of his time:

* He was probably the first to understand the function of the lens of the eye and to draw the connections between the eyeballs and optic nerves.
* He was one of the first to realize that the eye did not emit particles as the ancients had pronounced.

* He grasped that light behaved like a wave and reflected from different surfaces in different ways. Light and sound both travelled in what he called a 'tremor' – he described wave motion by observing how a blade of straw will be lifted by ripples on a sheet of water and yet remain in the same place.

* He realized that the sky was blue because of the effect of solar rays passing through the atmosphere – over 300 years before Lord Rayleigh described this effect in 1871.

* He distinguished between central and peripheral vision and was the first to write about the way the eyes function stereoscopically.

* He studied the reasons for long-sightedness (from which he suffered in the second half of his life), and experimented with lenses. He created an optical device that increased the field of vision by using a glass hemisphere full of water.

* He made an early type of telescope over a hundred years before it was developed by other scientists.

* He experimented with the 'camera obscura', an early forerunner of the camera, where light passes through a pinhole and creates an optical image on a flat surface.

ANATOMY

Another field of science in which Leonardo excelled was anatomy, which he saw as an essential aspect of study for the painter. He was the first to combine anatomy as both a science and an art – hitherto artists had always been interested in the external details of the body while the anatomist studied internal systems. Leonardo believed that anatomical drawings could relate a lot of information that was impossible to convey in words. He was right about this, for anatomical drawing has remained one of the most valuable teaching tools up to the present day. Leonardo studied the earlier anatomists, such as Galen, Avicenna (tenth to eleven centuries) and Mondino (thirteenth to fourteenth centuries) and he met top anatomists of his day. He worked a great deal from animal dissections, making increasingly meticulous drawings.

Human dissection was illegal, but he managed to dissect quite a lot of corpses in hospitals in Florence and Rome. He usually had to work secretively at night, which earned him accusations of necromancy, but he was so fascinated that he worked on regardless.

Dissecting corpses at night gave Leonardo the creeps.

Time was of the essence – there was no way of preserving corpses in those days and they became horribly smelly and potentially dangerous from the point of view of infection. Leonardo eventually produced hundreds of astoundingly accurate anatomical drawings, many of which are up to modern standards. Frequently the parts are drawn in exploded diagrams, showing how they all fit together – for example a series of cross-sections through a human leg.

Leonardo performed pioneering dissections on many parts of both animal and human bodies:

* He examined the structure of an ox brain by a method that he devised of filling the skull cavity with melted wax so as to make a cast.

* He drew cross-sections of the human skull and made accurate studies of most of the bones in the body, including pictures of the spine showing the correct curvature and number of bones.

* He also drew a whole series of studies of the muscular system, examining the muscles in many different positions and finding out exactly how they moved the bones of the skeleton.

* He dissected out some of the major nerves, and showed under-standing of the way the nervous system functioned when he commented that 'the nape' (back of the neck)' is the source of nerves eliciting the voluntary movement of limbs'.

* He investigated the major organs of the body, including the heart, lungs, liver, spleen and stomach. His anatomical drawings of these organs are astonishing, although his understanding of their functioning remained limited and he still based his ideas on classical theories.

* He investigated both male and female reproductive and genital organs and again made some extraordinarily accurate drawings. Embryology fascinated him and he managed to obtain a seven-month-old human foetus for study, although most of his drawings are based on animals. In around 1510–12 he produced a cross-section of a human uterus, showing the baby with its umbilical chord. From the same period are a series of drawings of the curled up foetus, shown from different angles, which are exceptionally advanced for Leonardo's times.

* One of his most well-known drawings, of a cross-section of a man and woman having sexual intercourse, was drawn in around 1493.

COMPOSITION

A painter had to give much attention to the composition of his pictures in order to achieve the desirable sense of harmony. He must think about where the figures were to be placed, and consider lighting, colours, poses, background and so on. Leonardo gives advice about all this in his notebooks. He strongly recommends that the student always return to the objects of nature, rather than slavishly copying the masters and possibly acquiring bad habits – 'he who can go to the fountain does not go to the water jar'. For example, when painting on a chapel wall he advises against the common practice of depicting several scenes one above another, saying that this is 'extreme folly'. He advises the student instead to put the foreground at eye level and then depict all the other scenes on gradually diminishing little hills and plains.

Before starting a composition he recommends an interesting mind-clearing technique of staring at a spotted or stony wall and allowing the thoughts to wander. In this way the creative faculties of the brain can be stimulated and the artist begins to conceive ideas for little scenes, figures in action and so on. Leonardo offers lengthy advice about how to depict a battle scene, studying the facial expressions of fear and horror, the effects of dust and smoke, the turmoil of rearing horses, men's hair streaming in the wind and the agony of death. This whole passage is graphically descriptive and reads more like a passage of creative writing than formal instruction to the student. He writes similar sections describing how to depict night, tempest and floods. The underlying theme here is 'man's impotence when face-to-face with the relentless laws of nature'.

* * * *SUMMARY* * * *

• Leonardo wrote a lot in his notebooks about an artist's training and the way in which he believed he should live his life.

• He frequently emphasized the importance of careful study of the natural world.

• His studies in the fields of optics and anatomy were far ahead of his time.

• Leonardo gave advice to students about how to set about composing a painting, emphasizing that originality and working from life were important.

8 The Final Years 1508–19

BACK TO MILAN

Towards the end of 1508, Leonardo finally left Florence to live once more in Milan. Charles d'Amboise, the governor of Milan on behalf of Louis XII, invited Leonardo back to Milan as part of an attempt at cultural revival, and became his patron. Back in Milan Leonardo was appreciated once more and he worked as a court painter, architect and general advisor, working on plans for town buildings and water engineering projects such as fountains, wells, canals, dams and drainage systems. He was once more in demand as a military engineer as well because there was a war between Milan and Venice. The notebooks suggest that he travelled extensively, but there is little evidence of exactly where he went. He probably visited the Alps and it is to this period that many of his notes about botany and geology belong, as well as studies about the effects of distance, smoke and mist. His interest in cartography also continued and he drew maps of many rivers, canals, valleys and lakes in northern Italy.

During the first months back in Milan, Leonardo became friends with Francesco Melzi, who was later to become his chief heir. Melzi was only 17 at the time, a beautiful boy who soon became Leonardo's new favourite, putting Salai's nose well and truly out of joint. Unlike Salai, Melzi was a talented painter and well educated.

The most famous of all Leonardo's paintings, *Mona Lisa* (Louvre, Paris), sometimes called *La Joconde*, is a portrait of an unknown lady and may have been painted during this period, although its date is uncertain. *Mona Lisa*'s enigmatic smile and watchful, intelligent expression have appealed to people ever since her portrait was first painted. Vasari reports that *Mona Lisa* once had rosy, living flesh, but the painting has presumably since discoloured. It has a strange air of brooding mystery, which Leonardo achieved by using the sfumato technique. The picture has been endlessly copied and parodied – one can see versions of it all over the world, frequently used for advertising and logos. The identity of the lady remains a mystery – the most far-fetched idea is that it was actually a disguised self-portrait, done as some sort of subtle joke.

ELABORATE PROJECTS

A garden for Charles d'Amboise

Charles d'Amboise asked Leonardo to design a garden for an urban villa that he was planning in Milan. Leonardo came up with a scheme to divert water from canals in the city to fill elaborate water-courses. These would fill miniature lakes and waterfalls to be used as wine coolers, as well as powering all kinds of interesting devices. There would be surprise fountains and water jets that would ambush ladies and sprinkle their gowns. There were even to be water-powered musical instruments and a water clock that rang the hours. Statues would be everywhere, with satyrs and fauns peeping out of the bushes. One area was to be covered in a fine copper mesh to make a big aviary that would be filled with exotic birds. Unfortunately, like so many of Leonardo's projects, the gardens remained a fantasy.

The Trivulzio monument

Charles d'Amboise died in 1511 and the government of Milan was handed over to two generals – Gaston de Foix and Gian Giacomo Trivulzio. Leonardo was commissioned to create a showy equestrian monument for Trivulzio, who ironically was the bitter enemy of Ludovico Sforza, Leonardo's former patron, who had also commis-sioned such a monument. Yet again the project was never actually completed and all that remains of it are drawings (Royal Library, Windsor, England). These show that Leonardo might have gone a little over the top this time with an incredibly ornate affair, showing a life-sized horse set on a huge base with classical columns. In the base was to be a sarcophagus containing the deceased, supported by six harpies with candelabra and surrounded by eight more figures.

A masquerade

From the same period is a series of sketches for a **masquerade** that took place around 1511–12. These show people in elaborate costumes. The most magical one presents a typical Leonardo enigma – it shows a woman sitting by a water-fall, pointing into the distance and wearing a mysterious, seductive expression.

> **KEYWORD**
>
> Masquerade, gathering where people dress up and assume disguises.

ROME

By the middle of 1512, Milan became chaotic as a mixture of Spaniards, Swiss, papal mercenaries and Venetians took over the city and the French were thrown out. Many artists and intellectuals were forced to escape. Leonardo hung on for another year and finally packed his bags again and set off for Rome, accompanied by Melzi, Salai and others. He was offered accommodation at the Vatican by Giuliano de Medici, who was brother to the latest Pope, Leo X, and was to become Leonardo's next patron. Leo was a lecher and a glutton, but also a great humanist and the atmosphere in Rome was liberal and wealthy. Raphael was also in Rome and so, unfortunately, was Michelangelo, who was busily lapping up kudos for painting the Cistine Chapel. Leonardo gradually became more withdrawn with all this competition, but he kept busy with various projects such as paintings and a design for a villa at Trivoli. He also worked in northern Italy as an architect and as a military and hydraulic engineer.

As always, Leonardo's private studies were very important to him. He busied himself with antiquities, drawing ruined temples and palaces and the Vatican's collection of Roman marbles. He also studied math-ematics, geometry and military architecture. Leonardo certainly had a sense of humour and he continued to provide amusement for other people with little jokes and puzzles. On one occasion he frightened the wits out of courtiers at the Vatican by fastening silver wings and horns to a lizard, turning it into a small but scary dragon. He created other strange animals out of wax that he somehow managed to pump full of air so that they floated along. Even more bizarre, he sometimes used concealed bellows to pump air into the intestines of an ox, inflating them to a vast size and crowding bemused visitors into a corner of the room.

Leonardo enjoyed a good practical joke.

As he neared the end of his life, Leonardo seems to have become progressively more brooding and obsessive. In his notebook he wrote, 'tell me if anything was ever done?' perhaps indicating a feeling of the futility of life. In 1512 he produced a self-portrait in which he looks rather like an Old Testament prophet, with long beard and grave face. Another cartoon, dated about 1513 shows an old man sitting down and leaning on a stick, head in hand and gazing sadly into space – maybe this was another self-portrait. He was haunted by apocalyptic visions and made disturbed drawings of floods and horsemen who rode the wind. The end of the world had been a fashionable idea at the end of the fifteenth century and so many people had fled to the hills to escape a possible deluge that parts of Germany had become almost deserted. Leonardo took the idea to heart and wrote horrid descriptions of terrified animals and people clinging hopelessly to disappearing hill tops, while boats, tables, beds and dead bodies swirled around in the rising waters. Drawings (now at Windsor, England) show scenes such as a whole mountain collapsing onto a stricken town. Clearly Leonardo felt helpless in the face of his own impending death and the relentless tide of human suffering.

LAST WORKS

St John the Baptist (c. 1515, Louvre, Paris)

This strange painting, supposedly John the Baptist, has delicately curling, neat, wavy hair, soft voluptuous flesh and an enigmatic feminine smile, reminiscent of *Mona Lisa*. His right hand points heavenwards, using the cryptic symbol so commonly shown in Leonardo's paintings. Yet again, Leonardo has left us with a teasing riddle – is this really the wild ascetic hermit who lived alone in the desert? Only the little reed cross that he holds in his left hand marks him out as John the Baptist. The figure is unmistakably androgynous and some people have suggested that he represents pagan eroticism rather than traditional Christian symbolism. Interestingly there is a second painting, showing a very similar figure, but this time the subject is Bacchus (Louvre, Paris), Greek god of wine, vegetation and fertility. Critics disagree as to whether this second painting is attributable to Leonardo and it is probably a later adaptation of the first, or a copy of a painting now lost. A third painting, shows *The Angel of the Annunciation* (c. 1505–7, Öffentliche Kunstsammlung, Basel) with the same flowing hair, pointing finger and gently smiling face. Again, this is probably a copy of an original Leonardo. Both angel and Baptist were heralds of mysterious events – but exactly what mysterious events Leonardo actually had in mind remains open to speculation.

AT THE FRENCH COURT

In January 1515 Louis XII, the French king, died and was succeeded by his cousin François I, a dashing young man of 20 who immediately set about recapturing Milan. Pope Leo X decided to keep on the right side of this

> **KEYWORD**
>
> Fleur-de-lis, heraldic lily, with three stems bound together at the base.

assertive and learned new king and arranged peace talks at Bologna. Giuliano de Medici commissioned Leonardo to make a centrepiece for the occasion, and he created a mechanical lion which walked along and then opened up to reveal a **fleur-de-lis** where its heart would have been. The lion symbolized Leo for the pope, but was also a pun on Leonardo's own name. The fleur-de-lis was the emblem of French royalty and its presence at the heart of the lion symbolized the peaceful union of the two great powers.

François took to Leonardo straight away and late in 1516 became his last patron, inviting him to live at Cloux, a manor house near the royal home at Amboise. The relationship between the two men was almost of a mythical nature. François was six feet tall, about nine inches taller than the average man of the times, and wore golden armour, so that he must have appeared like a great warrior king. He was also well educated and a great patron of the arts. Leonardo, who was by now an archetypal sage, with his long grey beard and his wealth of learning and experience, became his mentor. A tunnel connected their two residences, and they spent many long nights together, deep in conversation.

Leonardo still had an active mind right up to the last and in 1518 he designed a triumphal arch with royal emblems of salamander and ermine, to celebrate a royal wedding and the birth of François's son. In his role as 'engineer and architect of the king' he set about developing a plan for a new city called Romorantin. This was to be built along the lines of a Roman military city, with a central canal and streets and squares laid out on a grid pattern. There was a royal palace and a huge basin for staging mock naval battles. Work was begun on the city, but ground to a halt when an epidemic broke out. The ideas were not entirely wasted, however, because some of them were used in later French Chateaux.

Leonardo's health was failing by now and he was to have only two summers at Cloux. His eyesight was weak and he suffered from arthritis in his hands. Eventually he could no longer hold a brush or a pen and Francesco Melzi had to write down notes and add details to paintings for him. Salai, now well and truly out of favour, left for Milan never to return. Leonardo died at Cloux on 2 May 1519. Popular legend says that he died in François's arms, but this may not be true. He was buried at the Church of St Florentin in Amboise.

Few of Leonardo's pupils are well known today, nevertheless his influence in the world of art has been huge, spreading during the two centuries following his death as far afield as France, Spain, Italy, Germany and Flanders. Many artists derived from him the use of sfumato, and careful study of facial expression, body language, anatomy and proportion. His contributions in the fields of science and engineering were also immense. Altogether he was a man of astounding intellect and great mystery whose insights continue to fascinate people 500 years after his death.

∗ ∗ ∗ ∗ SUMMARY ∗ ∗ ∗ ∗

• Leonardo spent a final five years in Milan, where his patron was Charles d'Amboise, and here he produced some of his last paintings.

• He then spent a period in Rome, where his health began to fail and he became increasingly withdrawn and depressed.

• His final years were spent peacefully and happily in France at Cloux, where he became a close friend of the king, François I.

TIMELINE 1452–1519

1452	Leonardo is born near Vinci on 15 April.
c.1466–69	Apprenticed to Verrocchio in Florence.
1470–72	Paints angel in *The Baptism of Christ*.
1472	Made a member of the Florentine Guild of Painters.
1473	First known landscape drawing.
1476	Suspended sentence after accusation of homosexuality.
1478	First independent commission.
1481	Leaves Florence for Milan, to work for Ludovico Sforza.
1483	Contract for *The Virgin of the Rocks*.
1484	Plague in Milan.
1489	Commission for Sforza monument.
1490	'Festa del Paradiso' – grand pageant in Milan. Arrival of Salai.
c. 1495	Begins work on *The Last Supper*.
1499	Leaves Milan and travels to Mantua and Venice.
1500	Back to Florence.
c. 1501	Cartoon for *Virgin and Child with St Anne*.
1502	Travels with Cesare Borgia.
1503	Work begins on *The Battle of Anghiari*.
1508	Back to Milan.
1513	Leonardo leaves for Rome.
1514	Accused of necromancy and barred from hospital of San Spirito in Rome.
1517	Lives at Amboise in France, by invitation of François I.
1519	Leonardo dies on 2 May and is buried at Amboise.

GLOSSARY

Acoustics Relating to sound or the sense of hearing.

Alchemy An esoteric practice combining aspects of mysticism, magic, science and religion.

Allegory Story, poem, painting, etc., in which the meaning is represented symbolically.

Altarpiece Work of art set above or behind the altar in a church.

Anatomy Science investigating the structure of animals and plants.

Apothecary Chemist who dispenses medicine and drugs.

Ballistics Science of projectiles and firearms.

Bestiary Moralizing book about real and imaginary beasts.

Cartography Map-making.

Cartoon Full-sized drawing as a preliminary for a painting.

Ceramics Products made of clay and hardened by firing in a kiln.

Chiaroscuro Making sense of 3D in painting by using light and shade.

Contrapposto Twisted pose.

Cosmos The universe.

Dissection Cutting up dead plants or animals in order to investigate the structure and functions of their parts.

Empirical Deriving knowledge from experience rather than from theory or belief.

Esoteric Secret or mystical

Fleur-de-lis Heraldic lily, with three stems bound together at the base.

Fresco Water-colour painting done on a wall or ceiling while the plaster is still wet.

Geometry Branch of maths that studies points, lines, surfaces and solid shapes.

Gesso Plaster of Paris, or gypsum, used for sculpture and painting.

Hermetic To do with alchemy and other secret practices.

Humanism An outlook that is focused on the human rather than the divine or supernatural.

Hydraulics Science of how to transport water and use it as a power source.

Iconoclastic Attacking popular beliefs and destroying religious imagery such as paintings.

Logic The philosophy of reasoning.

Lunette Half-moon shaped space above a door or window, often containing a painting or sculpture.

Mannerism Style of Italian art characterized by elongated figures and twisted poses.

Masque A dramatic and musical entertainment.

Masquerade Gathering where people dress up and assume disguises.

Marquetry Decorative inlaid work using wood, ivory, etc.

Metaphysics The philosophy of mind and thought.

Mural Painting done directly onto a wall.

Necromancy Magic involving assistance from the spirits of the dead.

Omphalos The centre, or hub of something.

Optics Science investigating the eye and vision.

Pageant An elaborate staged spectacle or parade.

Perspective The art of drawing solid objects on a two-dimensional surface in such a way that they appear solid and real.

Philosophy A system of learning that investigates the underlying nature and truth of knowledge and existence.

Pigment Colouring used as paint or dye.

Polyhedra Solid figures, such as cubes, with many faces.

Putti (singular **putto**) a naked child, especially a cherub or cupid.

Renaissance A progressive cultural period which spanned the fourteenth to sixteenth centuries. It was characterized by a 're-birth' of classical thinking and a huge growth of new ideas in art, science, philosophy and writing.

Rhetoric The art of persuasive argument in speaking or writing.

Secco Technique of painting on dry plaster.

Secular Concerned with worldly affairs rather than the divine.

Sfumato Subtle modelling of forms in painting, using gradual transitions of light and shade.

Sonnet Poem with 14 lines and a formal rhyme scheme.

Stucco Type of plaster used for moulding and for coating surfaces.

Tempera Painting using a mixture of pigment and other substances.

Terracotta Unglazed, brownish-red earthenware.

Tondo A circular painting or relief design.

Transcript Written copy.

Vanishing point The point at which receding parallel lines seen in perspective appear to meet.

FURTHER READING

BIOGRAPHY

Giovio, Paolo. *Leonardi Vincii Vita.* c. 1527 Translated by Jean Paul Richter.

Gaddiano, Anonimo. *Codex Magliabecchiano.* c. 1530

Vasari, Giorgio. *Lives of the Artists. Volume 1.* Penguin. 1987. ISBN 01404 45005. (This is a translation taken from the second edition of Vasari's work, published in 1568.)

Clark, Kenneth. *Leonardo da Vinci.* Penguin. Revised version 1988, Martin Kemp. ISBN 01401 69822

LEONARDO'S NOTEBOOKS

Codex Arundel (British Library, London)

Codex Trivulzianus (Biblioteca Trivulziana, Milan)

Codex Atlanticus (Biblioteca Ambrosiana, Milan), so named because it was bound in the sixteenth century into an atlas-like form.

Codex on the flight of birds (Biblioteca Reale, Turin)

Codex Urbinas (Vatican Library, Rome)

Treatise on Painting (Vatican Library, Rome)

Two further important collections are:

Manuscripts A–M (Bibliothèque de l'Institute de France, Paris)

Windsor Castle Royal Library Collection (Windsor, England)

There are many further collections, notably in Madrid, London, Florence, New York and Venice.

The Notebooks of Leonardo da Vinci. Selected by Irma Richter. Oxford University Press.1952. Paperback version 1998. ISBN 01928 38970. A selection from the notebooks – one of the best introductory reads.

WHERE TO SEE LEONARDO'S WORK

Leonardo's work is now widely scattered in museums, art galleries and private collections all over Europe and the USA. Below are some of the places where you can see his paintings and drawings and find out more about him:

* Florence, Italy: Uffizi Gallery – *The Baptism of Christ, The Annunciation, The Adoration of the Magi.*

* Vinci, Italy: Museo Leonardiano – Huge collection of machines, models and reproductions of manuscripts; Bibliotecca Leonardiana – complete collection of reproductions of Leonardo's manuscripts; Anchiano, 3 km from Vinci – Leonardo's birthplace.

* Milan, Italy: Ambrosiana Library – *Portrait of a Musician*, drawings; Church of Santa Maria Delle Grazie – *The Last Supper.*

* Rome, Italy: Vatican Museum – *St Jerome.*

* London, England: National Gallery – *Virgin and Child with St Anne and John the Baptist, The Virgin of the Rocks* (second version); British Museum – Drawings of war machines and cartoons.

* Windsor, England: Windsor Castle Museum – Drawings.

* Paris, France: The Louvre – *The Virgin of the Rocks* (first version), *St John the Baptist, Mona Lisa, The Virgin and Child with St Anne*; Bibliothèque de l'Institute de France – Drawings.

INDEX

Adoration of the Magi 27–28

Alberti, Leone 21

d'Amboise, Charles 72

anatomy 68–70

Angel of the Annunciation 76

Annunciation, The 25

apocalypse 75–77

architecture 32–34

Aristotle 10

arts, the 61–62

Bacchus 76

Baptism of Christ, The 24–25

Battle of Anghiari, The 46–48

Benois Madonna 26

Boccaccio, Giovanni 11

Bondone, Giotto di 12–13

Borgia, Cesare 44–45

botany 64

Botticelli, Sandro 15

Brunelleschi, Filippo 13–14

cartography 45–46

Cecilia Gallerani 34

chiaroscuro 20

Cloux 77

Codex Atlanticus 50

colour 63–64

composition 70–71

contrapposto 20

cosmos 50–53

Donatello 13

draperies 65–66

Duchy of Milan 29–31

early life and family 4–6

engineering 32–34

d'Este, Isabella 39–41

Euclid 10

expression of the spirit 66

Festa del Paradiso 30

flight 55–56

Florence 18–19

François I 77

Gaddiano, Anonimo 4

Galen 10

geometry 63

Ginevra de Benci 25–26

Giovio, Paolo 3

Last Supper, The 36–37

Leda and the Swan 43

light and shadow 63–64

Louis XII 77

Machiavelli, Niccolo 16–17

machines 53–55

Madonna with the Carnation 26

Madonna with the Yarn Winder 42–43

mannerism 17

Masaccio 14

masquerade 74

mechanical lion 77

Medici, Lorenzo de 19–20

Melzi, Francesco 50

Michelangelo 16

Milan 29–30

Mona Lisa 72–73

movement 65

music 34

nature, working from 22–23

Neptune 42

notebooks 49–52

optics and perspective 66–68

Pacioli, Luca 39

Perugino, Pierro 21

Petrarch 11

Plato 11

Pollaiuolo, Antonio 15, 21

Portrait of a Musician 34

proportion 65

Raphael 16

Renaissance 1, 8–17

Robbia, Andrea della 14

Rome 74–76

Romorantin 77–79

Saint Jerome Penitent 27

Salai, Giacomo 31

self-portrait 75

Sforza monument 29–31

Sforza, Ludovico 29–30

sfumato 22

St John the Baptist 76

stories and wisdom 56–59

Toscanelli, Paolo 21

treatise on painting 61

Trivulzio monument 73

vanishing point 13

Vasari, Giorgio 4

Venice 40

Verrocchio, Andrea del 20–21

Vinci 5–6

Virgin and Child with St Anne 43–44

Virgin of the Rocks, The 35–36

GANDHI –
A BEGINNER'S GUIDE

Genevieve Blais

Gandhi – A Beginner's Guide invites you to take a glimpse into the life of this profound character. Follow his extraordinary quest for morality, justice and spirituality and discover how his strategy of passive resistance achieved social reform. Find out how his influence has now extended far beyond the barriers of a nation.

Genevieve Blais's compelling text investigates:

- Gandhi's background and the times he lived in
- Britain's role in the history of India
- the events leading up to and prior to the Salt March
- Gandhi's role in the independence of India
- his assassination and legacy.

The facts … the concepts … the ideas …

CHARLES DARWIN – A BEGINNER'S GUIDE

Gill Hands

Charles Darwin – A Beginner's Guide introduces you to the man whose scientific observations on evolution challenged the religious beliefs of Victorian society, but which are now generally accepted as being perfectly logical. Examine the historical perspective of evolution and the various philosophical questions that arise. No need to wrestle with difficult concepts as key ideas are presented in a clear jargon-free way.

Gill Hands' informative text explores:

- ■ Darwin's background and the times he lived in
- ■ the development of the theory of natural selection
- ■ the scientific basis for evolution
- ■ the relevance of his ideas in today's world.

The facts … the concepts … the ideas …

SARTRE – A BEGINNER'S GUIDE

George Myerson

Sartre – A Beginner's Guide introduces you to the life and work of this leading novelist, central philosopher and major dramatist. Sartre remains a symbol of the committed writer and thinker, and his existentialism continues to challenge us.

George Myerson's fascinating introduction:

- brings the different phases of Sartre's thought and art to life
- explains the key ideas of Sartre's existentialism using examples from his work
- summarises essential information about characters, plots and arguments in the major works
- puts Sartre in philosophical and historical context.

The facts … the concepts … the ideas …

ISAAC NEWTON – A BEGINNER'S GUIDE

Jane Jakeman

Isaac Newton – A Beginner's Guide introduces you to the towering genius. Explore how his science revolutionized our world and his philosophy changed our thought. Find out more about Newton the man, and as scientist, philosopher, alchemist and respected public figure.

Jane Jakeman's lively text;

- describes Newton's background and the times he lived in
- explores his scientific ideas and their effect on our lives
- delves into the character of the man
- examines the influence of Newton on his own time and today.

The facts ... the concepts ... the ideas ...